REREADING LITERATURE
Emily Brontë

REREADING LITERATURE
General Editor: Terry Eagleton

Alexander Pope
Laura Brown

Charles Dickens
Steven Connor

Emily Brontë
James H. Kavanagh

Emily Brontë

James H. Kavanagh

Basil Blackwell

© James H. Kavanagh 1985

First published 1985

Basil Blackwell Ltd
108 Cowley Road, Oxford, OX4 1JF, UK

Basil Blackwell Inc.
432 Park Avenue South, Suite 1505,
New York, NY 10016, USA

British Library Cataloguing in Publication Data

Kavanagh, James H.
    Emily Brontë — (Rereading literature)
    1. Brontë, Emily Wuthering Heights
    I. Title   II. Series
    823'.8   PR4172.W73

    ISBN 0–631–13506–5
    ISBN 0–631–13507–3 Pbk

Library of Congress Cataloging in Publication Data

Kavanagh, James H. 1948 —
    Emily Brontë.
    (Rereading literature)|
    Includes index.
    I. Brontë, Emily, 1818–1848. Wuthering Heights.
    I. Title.   II. Series.
    PR4172.W73K3 1985 823'.8   84–28409
    ISBN 0–631–13506–5
    ISBN 0–631–13507–3 (pbk.)

Typeset by Cambrian Typesetters, Frimley, Surrey
Printed in Great Britain by Whitstable Litho Ltd, Kent

To
Ellen A. Howard (1882?—1981), my grandmother,
Mary Howard Kavanagh, my mother,
and Nora Fallon (18??—1971), my nurse—
from whom I learned
strength.

And to E.M., C.D., and S.G.,
who taught me more.

Contents

Editor's Preface

'Vision', 'transcendental imagination', 'timeless value', 'cosmic energy': such are the terms in which criticism has become accustomed to discussing the fiction of the Brontës, the three weird sisters deposited upon the Yorkshire moors from some metaphysical outer space. The effect of such rhapsodic language is to block any attempt to think through these novels in relation to the real historical world in which they are rooted, encouraging instead the demeaning notion of the Brontë sisters as freaks, literary accidents, some unaccountable natural phenomenon which, like a storm or a sunset, is to be admired rather than analysed. Yet the sisters were no strangers to sexual oppression, social violence, cultural insecurity and material deprivation, themes which permeate their work from end to end and which, as James Kavanagh argues here in the case of *Wuthering Heights*, shape its very inner substance. The celebrated Brontëan 'imagination' is not dissociable from these apparently more drab matters — though it is remarkable how tenaciously modern criticism has clung to the Romantic delusion that there is indeed some single, distinguishable human faculty known as 'the imagination', as enduring and identifiable as the left foot or the right cortex.

James Kavanagh finds nothing in the least timeless about the values of *Wuthering Heights*, and nothing at all 'transcendental' about its vision. Indeed part of the proper scandalousness of his study lies in its sense of just how unerringly *precise*, how specific to certain definite social preoccupations, the whole rich project of Emily's novel actually is. Faithful to the productive hypothesis that literary works are less *objects* than *strategies*, complex symbolic devices for managing certain often intolerable conflicts in historical experience itself, Kavanagh offers the reader a *Wuthering Heights* which is, in more than one sense of the word, a *plot*. The plot consists in an attempt to bring to provisional resolution an unwelcome contradiction at the heart of capitalist and patriarchal society: the deeply embarrassing fact that just as the industrial capitalist system needs to mobilize energies which it also seeks to suppress, so the institution of the family is founded upon a potentially anarchic force — sexual desire itself — which it must nevertheless strictly regulate. *Wuthering Heights* is an 'answer', albeit tentative and in some ways ambiguous, to these most material of dilemmas; by casting them in richly symbolic form it struggles towards 'discharging' these pent-up tensions and bringing characters, narrative and reader to a kind of rest.

All strategies require individual agents for their execution; and for Kavanagh the novel's chief protagonists, those who steer and stage-manage its overall design, are not Catherine and Heathcliff but, rather surprisingly, Heathcliff and Nelly Dean. It should be confessed right away that to argue this intriguing case Kavanagh draws upon the resources of that most unEnglish and unnerving of theories, Freudian psychoanalysis. For those who believe themselves to have common sense rather than an unconscious, this approach may prove at times a little unpalatable; yet it allows Kavanagh to produce a powerfully persuasive reading of the text, one prepared to be a little more detailed and specific about the nature of sexual desire than nebulous critical talk of 'passion' or 'eternal love'. Heathcliff, in this reading, figures less as Catherine's lover than as her 'Oedipal father': he is, as Kavanagh demonstrates, a substitute father for her, but one who actually expresses the sexual desire for the daughter which the real father must repress. Nelly Dean, by contrast, figures as the 'phallic mother', as the sign of maternal power and social authority, agent and upholder of the social and sexual Law, which intervenes to forbid such tabooed incestuous relationships. Heathcliff and Nelly, then, square up to one another as violent antagonists on that battlefield which is Catherine's body, the one attempting to seduce her by the 'anarchy of desire', the other striving to rescue her for patriarchy and social respectability by a 'sadistic control'.

In the end, neither antagonist achieves unqualified victory; and each, as Kavanagh shows, is forced to resort in some sense to the stratagems of the other. Nelly is the successful instrument by which, after the lawless disruptions of a Heathcliff, the patriarchal family is pieced painfully together again, Law re-established, the Earnshaw lineage secured, and the legitimate process of sexual reproduction — the bourgeois family — perpetuated. But this resolution can be attained only at the cost of a sharp separation of the stable, authoritarian family from that more restless, ceaselessly mobile world of socially and sexually productive energy which Heathcliff has come to symbolize. Though Heathcliff himself is conveniently (and *necessarily*) killed off in this denouement, the shadow of what he signifies — a tragically unappeasable desire, which is both the furious dynamism of the capitalist and the rage for full recognition of the oppressed worker — falls disquietingly across the novel's final settlement, to underline the precariousness of all social order. The dilemma faced by capitalist and patriarchal society — how is one to maintain ideological stability in a society whose very social, sexual and economic life-blood is desire, appetite, restless transformation? — is resolved by dividing off the family, space of authority and tranquillity, from the wider political society, severing sexual from social reproduction.

All these issues leave their mark on the novel's curious form. For if that form is on the one hand profoundly unstable, with its Chinese-box effects of texts-within-texts, narratives of narratives, it is also rigorously 'framed', in more than one sense of the term, by the dominative narrative control of Nelly herself. To narrate is to exercise power, not least when, as with Nelly, it involves a tendentious editing and revising of others' interpretations; and Kavanagh sees it as part of the work's incorporative strategy that Heathcliff, the 'Romantic' voice of the text, is himself 'uttered' and encompassed by that very different voice of sober bourgeois realism which is Nelly's.

It is perhaps not surprising, given the surname of the author of this study, that he should note at one point a tantalizing indication that Heathcliff is quite probably Irish. A byword for wretchedness and 'savagery', a perennial object of British mockery and brutality, the Irish, like Heathcliff, have shown themselves no strangers to violent rebellion over the miserable centuries of their subjugation. Could it be that in our own time, when an ambivalently destructive and emancipatory force from that quarter is once more locked in tragic conflict with a repressive Law, Heathcliff, still unappeased, sleeps unquietly in his grave?

Terry Eagleton

Preface

There are two 'gaps' that make this book precarious, and at the same time make it possible. One is the distance between everyday 'natural' language and the language of contemporary criticism. Much of what we now understand as traditional criticism implicitly assumes a common language (representing common values), which grounds it, the literature upon which it comments, and readers of both. Thus, traditional criticism can appeal to its readers on the basis of a presumed 'common sense' language that facilitates communication.

There are many versions of contemporary critical theory, by no means all of a piece; every version, however, has the great disadvantage of recognizing the specificity and peculiarity of its language, which means it is always asking its readers to do the same. The theoretical framework of my critical practice certainly tends to see 'common sense' as, in large part, a convenient designation for the most firmly established cultural conventions, and 'common sense' language as the unavoidable jargon of the dominant ideology. It asserts that the analysis of literature and culture — of such non-trivial problems as the relation between subjectivity and social order, narrative and the unconscious, psychology and economy — is a task no less difficult, and no less demanding of a specialized language, than the study of sub-atomic particles or mammalian respiratory systems.[1] This can sometimes make communication difficult in a field where *liking* an object is so often confused with *studying* it. Students (and scholars) do not tend to expect every presentation of relativity theory to be easily comprehensible to anyone who enjoys gazing at the stars, in the way that they often expect every piece of literary criticism to be transparent for anyone who enjoys reading novels and poems. Part of the point of contemporary literary theory, as I understand it, is that there is a similarly irreducible difference in both cases.

Of course, though difficult and asking to be understood on its own terms, a critical discourse can be comprehensible, can facilitate the transition between 'normal' and unavoidably specialized languages, and should certainly make an attempt to give the reader a return for the effort demanded. These are pedagogical — even political — problems and responsibilities that I should not wish to ignore. I have tried in this book to avoid what I think is the shortcoming of some contemporary criticism that can make it seem perversely obscurantist — namely, carelessness and inconsistency in the use of terminology. Accordingly, I have tried to define unfamiliar terms when they are first used, and to use them consistently throughout.

This will still not eliminate all of the difficulty many readers might experience with my critical prose, however. Those not versed in new critical languages may feel that, for example, 'literary producer' is just a more complicated, pretentious expression for 'author', that there is a constant use of 'strange' new words in place of 'ordinary' old words that mean exactly the same thing. But this is never just a question of different *words* (or it would not produce such discomfort!); it is always also a question of different *languages*, different semantic contexts in which particular words refer to other words and concepts that support, in fact, very different *meanings*. (In the example, the word 'author' is 'ordinarily' given a meaning by Romantic, expressivist notions of 'creativity' and 'genius', while the term 'literary producer' would take a different kind of meaning from the putatively materialist notions of literature as a mode of ideological production that support it.)

I cannot abolish all the difficulty of my own prose, because I cannot supply the entire semantic context that supports many of my formulations — a context that includes the specialized language of psychoanalysis, structuralist and post-structuralist textual theory, and contemporary Marxism. I can explain those few elements that are crucial to this essay, and refer the reader to sources that provide further elaboration. If I use formulations that resonate with these theoretical languages, this is in the hope that they will provoke the reader to further investigation. I think that a necessary part of the critical project in which this monograph participates is the development of a style, as different from the 'plain' style of criticism, perhaps, as is modernist from 'realist' prose, a dense and resonant style that continually foregrounds the difference between text and criticism which makes the latter possible. Whether my particular contribution to this effect is successful depends, of course, on whether the reader feels, as I hope s/he will, that the reading of Emily Brontë made possible by this strategy is indeed full and persuasive.

Another gap, and a more disturbing burden of difference, is inscribed in the very attempt to do a systematic analysis of Emily Brontë's work. It seems to me, as it must to anyone, that there is an element of arrogance in such a project. By what right, and in what language, does a late twentieth-century male launch into an ostensibly exhaustive theoretical anatomy of the writing of an early-Victorian woman? One can no longer blithely ignore the differences these questions imply. They are enormous, and demand acknowledgement.

One way of approaching this question is to point out that we always talk/write about ourselves. This work, therefore, would be first of all an attempt to address questions of critical theory, of the relation of feminism and historical materialism, of history and the unconscious, that are visible and pressing for contemporary readers in a way that they could not be for Emily Brontë; through our formulation of those questions, then, we might produce an understanding of Emily Brontë's work of a kind that she could not have. The only reason to do any of this is for the knowledge, the help, that it gives us. I find this type of response valid. It recognizes the distance between a discourse and its object that is necessary to know anything about the object; and it recognizes that in that distance, something *can* be known.

What I do not believe, and do not want to suggest, is that my work or any other can effectively abolish that difference. I make what I hope to be a cogent, but by no means final or complete, statement. We can accept the illusion — because it's not just an illusion — that, if we work hard, even the most unbridgeable gap can be crossed. Something that Emily Brontë has done, after all, has in some circuitous arc jumped quite a gap to touch this twentieth-century male. I can write about Emily Brontë, I suppose, because she can still write to me. But however nicely, and with whatever sparks, that gap is crossed or filled, it quickly opens up again, to offer an even greater difference, to beckon yet another question, always leaving us on the other side.

If we can write about Emily Brontë, that is only because we traverse, and are thrown back across, greater distances every day:

> Takver woke at dawn. She leaned on her elbow and looked across Shevek at the grey square of the window, and then at him. He lay on his back, breathing so quietly that his chest scarcely moved, his face thrown back a little, remote and stern in the thin light. We came, Takver thought, from a great distance to each other. We have always done so. Over great distances, over years, over abysses of chance. It is because he comes from so far away that nothing can separate us. Nothing, no distances, no years, can be greater than the distance that's already between us, the distance of our sex, the difference of our being, our minds;

that gap, that abyss which we bridge with a look, with a touch, with a word, the easiest thing in the world. Look, how far away he is, asleep. Look how far away he is, he always is. But he comes back, he comes back, he comes back . . .[2]

Acknowledgements

I would like to thank the Princeton University English Department for providing me with the pleasant material and professional conditions necessary to complete this work. Among my colleagues who provided more intangible forms of support, I am thankful to Val Smith and Dave Van Leer, who always listened to the most irrelevant frustrations, and to Elaine Showalter and Jules Law, whose suggestions and comments on the specific topic of this book helped me to turn some corners. My intellectual debt to Jane Gallop is apparent in what follows; any distortions of her work are, of course, my responsibility. In the background of this book, less visible but no less important, lurks the influence of Gayatri Spivak, which I gratefully acknowledge.

There is one acknowledgement that I do not have to make, although its absence should be mentioned, since it is the mark of a significant change in the way intellectual work is produced. There is no patient, untiring typist or clerical assistant to be thanked. This book was composed entirely on a screen, using Waterloo Script running on an IBM 3081, with the final typescript produced on an IBM 6670 Model II laser printer. Those readers who do not know what I am talking about, soon will. Of course, I have ambivalent feelings about the significance of this fact: on the one hand, it marks the beginning of the end of another cottage industry upon which many marginal workers —

mostly women — depend; on the other hand, it means that no woman or man — so often an unpaid spouse or companion — wasted a few hundred hours of her or his life being my personal secretary. But my feelings about this matter little, since it is the symptom of a new wave of capitalist rationalization of office work that, now that its effects are felt in the higher social spheres of academia, has already become irreversible. I must, however, acknowledge the assistance of the professional and technical staff of the Princeton University Computer Center, about whom I can have no illusion that they laboured out of love of myself or my project.

My son, Ian, is perhaps the only person who lost something from my writing this book. I cannot give back the time, but I can give him my thanks and love, and hope that one day he will retrieve some value from what I have done.

Fredric Jameson saw this work through its initial stages some years ago, while he was also seeing me through the more difficult stages of my own personal 'cultural revolution'. His sympathetic, capacious interrogation of the various schools of contemporary literary theory provides a model that all of us who pretend to some version of critical Marxism can only hope imperfectly to imitate. It is no small feat to have been single-handedly responsible for having re-established the legitimacy of Marxism within the American literary academy, and it is no small honour to have benefited from his work as a student and friend.

I cannot sufficiently acknowledge my debt to Solange Guénoun who had a profound effect on the thinking that went into this book, and gave me indispensable help with the revisions. More perhaps than she might like to know, she has been an influence, a support and an ally.

Everyone in this profession knows, and has been touched by, the work of Terry Eagleton. My debt to him as a mentor and colleague is obvious. I have also had the fortune to know him as a friend and comrade. I only hope that with this book I can return some of his affection and support.

Introduction: *Wuthering Heights* and Critical Method

Emily Brontë has always been a peculiar figure in the English literary pantheon. Her reputation rests entirely on a single novel, *Wuthering Heights*, which has itself been treated as a rather odd literary specimen.[1] A member of a troubled family whose three daughters emerged suddenly on to the nineteenth-century literary scene, embarrassing it with their talent, Emily has now come to be seen as a less respectable author than her more prolific sister Charlotte, while somewhat more successful than her younger sister Anne. The result has been that Anne's work has gone largely unread, Charlotte's work has become a staple of the undergraduate English curriculum, and Emily's 'strange book' has continued to fascinate readers while perplexing critics.

Critical confusion about Emily's work began with contemporary reviews of *Wuthering Heights*, which spoke uncomfortably of the novel as 'a strange book . . . not entirely without evidences of considerable power: but, as a whole . . . wild, confused, disjointed, and improbable',[2] with characters who 'are so new, so wildly grotesque, so entirely without art, that they strike us as proceeding from a mind of limited experience, but of original energy, and of a singular and distinctive cast'.[3]

Confusion was exacerbated by the male pseudonyms under which the Brontës chose to publish their first works, motivated, as Charlotte wrote, by 'a vague impression that authoresses are liable to be looked on with prejudice; we had noticed how critics sometimes use for their chastisement the weapon of personality, and for their reward, a flattery, which is not true praise.'[4] This 'impression' was sharply confirmed by the inconsistency of reviewers — or rather, their *consistency* according to a gender-determined double standard. Thus, even disapproval of *Wuthering Heights* was initially tempered, in many critics who thought they were confronting a male author, by a kind of grudging admiration for the courage with which the story plunged into the unknown:

> We detest the affectation and effeminate frippery which is too frequent in the modern novel, and willingly trust ourselves with an author who goes at once fearlessly into the moors and desolate places, for his heroes; but we must at the same time stipulate with him that he shall not drag into the light all that he discovers, of coarse and loathsome, in his wandering.[5]

When its female authorship was recognized, critical attitudes tended to change from camaraderie to condescension. The writer was chided for her lack of mature feminine discretion, and her novel was seen as 'the flight of an impatient fancy fluttering in the very exultation of its young wings ... The authoress has too often disgusted, where she should have terrified, and has allowed us a familiarity with her fiend [Heathcliff] which had ended in unequivocal contempt.'[6]

In sum, Emily Brontë's novel was from the first acknowledged as a work of strange power and energy, but was also found to be dangerously 'excessive': too much passion, too much violence, even too many narrators. A kind of literary changeling, '*Wuthering Heights* must have seemed to Emily's contemporaries an English novel without ancestors, as it seems now to be almost without descendants.'[7]

Indeed, much modern criticism also seems to find Emily Brontë's novel 'a world of brilliant figures in an atmo-

sphere of mist . . . the "large utterance" of a baby god'.[8]
As the effort to mythologize overcame the impulse to
moralize, the dominant twentieth-century strategy for
interpreting *Wuthering Heights* has been to generate critical
schemes that attempt to mirror, or re-evoke, what is seen
as the transcendent mystery of the text. In a well-known
essay, which became a paradigm for much of the later
criticism, Lord David Cecil developed what we might call
the cosmology of *Wuthering Heights*. He saw the novel as
'a microcosm of the universal scheme as Emily Brontë
conceived it' — that is, as a fierce clash between 'the land
of the storm' (the Heights) on one side, and the 'home of
calm' (the Grange) on the other.[9] Following Cecil, some
critics responded with awe, even fear, at the 'transcendent,
supersexual relationship'[10] at the centre of the turmoil.
Cathy and Heathcliff were seen as 'demonic beings . . .
mythical powers, nearly, in their identification with an uncompromising . . . cosmic force',[11] or as representing 'the
raw, inhuman reality of anonymous natural energies . . .
disrupting all around them with their monstrous appetite
for an inhuman kind of intercourse'.[12]

This critical strategy of turning Emily Brontë into a
kind of perverse Mother Nature, and her work into a
cosmic meteorological phenomenon, as stunning and in-
explicable as some galactic storm, reaches an epitome in
Winifred Gérin's commentary on *Wuthering Heights*:

> Concerned with eternal principles of life, death, love
> and immortality, it has a timeless quality that puts it
> far nearer to such a work as *The Faery Queen* than to
> any contemporary Victorian novel. It has no concern
> for social questions, but is an expression of primitive
> passions, of the elemental forces in Man and Nature
> that the author shows as connecting all Creation. Hers
> is a cosmic vision that has little to do with nineteenth-
> century materialism. At the same time the narrative is
> firmly set in the soil. The chronological framework of
> the plot is precise; the seasonal changes meticulously

noted, but rather as might be done by men in space who are removed from the world's orbit. The people moving in the spacious panorama of the moorlands are seen with the sharp focus of the dreamer who notes all the details of his dream but cannot account for them. No one questions the action of *Wuthering Heights*; it is far too compelling to be explained and is invested throughout with the unequivocal nature of supernatural vision, the same that informs Emily Brontë's poetry. Yet the houses and interiors are as homely as a Dutch painting. Nothing could be less 'fey' than Emily Brontë's Yorkshire kitchens, cobbled stableyards, labouring servants. It is the naturalness of *Wuthering Heights* that heightens its dream-like quality (for everyone knows that dreams are deceptively realistic in detail), and that makes its spiritual daring unique. In this respect the book is the perfect mirror of the author's mind, since it reflects her own exceptional ability to live on two planes of consciousness at one and the same time.

For the reader who finds *Wuthering Heights* a perplexing book to understand, it is useless to recommend critical commentary or analysis of its elusive pattern; the only key to its secret lies in the poetry Emily Brontë was writing. . . . Universal Oneness is the central theme of the poems as of *Wuthering Heights*.[13]

I quote Gérin at length because her language so neatly displays the convoluted strategies with which an idealist, 'common-sense' criticism manages and pacifies a 'difficult' text like *Wuthering Heights*. The immanence of a particular social world in the novel is duly noted, and then its significance is firmly denied; the novel is said finally to have no relation to 'social questions' concerning this world it so carefully imagines, but to be bound only to 'eternal principles'. Its concrete, contemporary naturalism is overshadowed by the 'timeless' quality it shares with other literary texts, generically and historically even more distant from the conditions of its production. Its 'dream-like' quality is found to be impossible to analyse, except through the magically direct access that this critic can give the reader to the famous 'author's mind' — assumed to be the ground of all literary significance. Gérin's critical tableau provides a particularly clear example of what Catherine Belsey calls the 'expressive realist' assumption — namely, 'that literature reflects the *reality* of experience as it is perceived by one (especially gifted) individual, who *expresses* it in a discourse which enables other individuals to recognise it as true'.[14]

Louis Althusser writes of ideology as ' "representing" for individuals an imaginary relation to their real conditions of existence'.[15] This relation works on, and imaginarily resolves, or even renders invisible, specific psychosexual as well as socio-historical tensions. Ideology thus helps to reproduce a given set of social relations by 'producing' individuals — or what Althusserian theory would call 'social subjects' — who have class and gender identities that seem coherent, and are appropriate to their place in the social order. In any culture, language is the most pervasive and elaborate semiotic system, or system of meaningful signs, with which individual subjects articulate their relation to collective social projects.[16] Literature is thus an important part of a society's ideological 'work' in the sense we have described, forming what we can call a 'semio-ideological' practice, a practice that experiments with the relations between subjectivity and society through the dense and powerful medium of language. Emily Brontë's literary work is also and inevitably an ideological, or semio-ideological, work in this sense, attempting to resolve intense, 'lived' personal and social contradictions.[17] The traces of the imperfect and peculiar textual joints that help make a new imaginary fit, also make the text susceptible to a 'symptomatic reading', a reading that can make visible the semes and seams where the text works most carefully to efface conflict.[18]

Similarly, a criticism like Gérin's can also be called

ideological, in the precise sense that it provides an imaginary resolution to the real contradictions of the authorial labour and textual effect ostensibly under consideration — a new perfect fit between reader, text, author and 'reality'. A self-confirming dialogue with a purportedly 'real' authorial mind reveals the 'secret' of the text, and unifies all its disparate strands and centrifugal forces under the sign of something called 'Universal Oneness'. This shift into accepting the text at the level of abstract mythology offers a pseudo-explanatory embrace that finally smothers the text's scandalous psycho-sexual power, which nineteenth-century critics correctly perceived as undermining the ideological pacification mechanisms expected in any novel, let alone that of a parson's daughter.

As Pierre Macherey and Etienne Balibar suggest, this kind of critical work can be understood as 'resuming' or repeating, rather than explaining, the ideological work of the text whose address it echoes; this parallels the psychiatric situation, where the analysand's account of the dream is not an explanation but a re-production of the dream, working on, and working out, the same unconscious conflicts: 'it is the same ideological conflicts, resulting in the last instance from the same historical contradictions, or from their transformations, that produce the form of the text and its commentaries.'[19] Theoretically, such an account of the dream or text is not outside of, but is within, and in fact helps to constitute, the dream or text 'itself'. This criticism therefore helps to 'produce' the text in a specific form. If we are to explain Emily Brontë's work, we cannot efface the violence, the contradiction, the sense of transgression, which mark its troubled discourse. Nor can we ignore the ways in which criticism already offers the novel to us in a discursive frame that 'presents' it precisely in an imaginary, and imaginarily coherent, relation to its real conditions of existence, and to the conflicted literary-ideological work that produced it.

The twentieth-century's cosmology of Emily Brontë's work has developed in a reciprocally reinforcing relation to the standard legend of her life — a vision of the shy, isolated Romantic consciousness, secluded from 'social questions' in the protected world of the Haworth parsonage. Charlotte's testimony that Emily 'had scarcely more practical knowledge of the peasantry amongst whom she lived, than a nun has of the country people who sometimes pass her convent gates' seems to sanction this legend. Yet, in the same paragraph, Charlotte also makes the somewhat countervailing point that Emily 'knew them: knew their ways, their language, their family histories; she could hear of them with interest, and talk of them with detail, minute, graphic, and accurate'.[20] Emily, then, at the very least, actively observed and thought about the social world in which she lived — a world that was buffeted not only by the winds on the moors to which the legend would draw all our attention. Nor should we ignore the ironic significance of Charlotte's remarks: there is much to be said about the powerful and disturbing cathexes that shape the inner life of a nun in her cloister.[21]

The standard critical hagiography, then, seems to leave us with an author who is far from an appropriate subject for an analysis informed by historical materialism. Yet there have been numerous Marxist analyses of *Wuthering Heights*, by no means confined to the quite proper effort to restore the novel's 'historical context'.[22] David Wilson's conspicuously ignored essay was one of the first to challenge the legend of an Emily Brontë living in a state of asocial reverie.[23] Wilson sought to restore a more realistic sense of the socio-historical conjuncture in which Emily Brontë lived and wrote, a conjuncture which, after all, supported the publication of the *Communist Manifesto* within a few months of *Wuthering Heights*.[24] Wilson succeeded admirably in this traditional Marxist historicizing approach, and his essay can be seen as a kind of alternative paradigm, providing a model for 'sociological' criticism analogous to Lord Cecil's model for 'mythological' criticism. If Wilson's work has been carefully forgotten, while Cecil's has been abundantly anthologized, it is not because 'sociological' criticism suffers in the comparison.

Wilson's demystification of the Haworth parsonage, his reconstruction of the class turmoil and religious-political strife in which Patrick Brontë was actively involved, his reminder of the mass uprisings which tore through the Brontës' immediate neighbourhood during Emily's formative years, his evocation of the suffering and resentment in the workers' faces that the Brontës confronted constantly in the streets of their village during the 'Hungry Forties' — these elements are prerequisite not just to some narrowly construed 'sociology of literature', but to any criticism that pretends to a comprehensive understanding of the conditions of Emily Brontë's literary practice.

Whatever Emily's imaginary identification with a Romanticized Nature, she actually lived in the midst of a turbulent capitalist society. Luddite machine-wrecking was sweeping through Yorkshire when Patrick Brontë first arrived in the West Riding. Haworth itself was in an area that witnessed the growing misery of thousands of weavers, whose manual cottage labour suddenly became worthless with the advent of mechanization. During Emily's youth, masses of these displaced and destitute workers passed through the towns, and there was rebellion as well as suffering. Emily's tenure as a governess in Halifax, for example, coincided with the Poor Law riots in the town. In 1842, the 'Plug' strikers passed through Haworth, building a movement that spread throughout the north, and ended in what Wilson calls 'a phase of guerilla warfare'.[25] Emily's father was fiercely partisan during these events. As a young Orangeman in Ireland, he had helped crush the Irish rebellion of 1789, and when he arrived in Yorkshire, in Hartshead, he took up arms in the militia of the Reverend Hammond Roberson,[26] known as 'the clerical dragon', to help suppress the Luddite rebellions. It was at this time that the Reverend Brontë purchased a pair of pistols, and began the habit of carrying a loaded firearm in his pocket and sleeping with one loaded *and* cocked near his bed.[27] As Gérin says, he 'lived in a mental state of siege raised only by his death'.[28] Thus, the state of Nature in Haworth and its environs was at least as much like that of Hobbes as that of Wordsworth.

The 'pistol' merits some attention, since it seems to be a peculiarly privileged index of Emily's relation to her father — a weapon/signifier that occasions some of the more revealing and 'symptomatic' comments in her biographies. Patrick made a conscientious effort to pass on his firing skills to his daughter, and their common target practice becomes an image of the 'new closeness [that] grew up in the year of their isolation together',[29] or even of how 'Emily had indeed become, for Patrick, the son he had so longed for.'[30] Gérin finds that 'To cock his pistol nightly in case of alarm, and to discharge it in the morning from his bedroom window, was a normal operation in his view for a gentleman with a pack of women to defend', and that, when his eyesight began to falter, 'Mr. Brontë realised the good sense of teaching Emily to fire, in case the need to protect the household should ever arise.' It is not clear here who is protecting whom, but this is certainly an indication of the liberality with which the Reverend Brontë encouraged his daughter's access to another token — along with what Sandra Gilbert and Susan Gubar identify as the 'deadly' pen[31] — of phallic power.

But perhaps the last word on Emily-Father-gun is to be found in the testimony of John Greenwood, the Haworth stationer, whose diary records, with what is surely one of the most remarkable parapraxes in Brontë literature,[32] that:

Mr. Brontë . . . had such unbounded confidence in his daughter Emily, knowing as he did, her unparalleled intrepidity and firmness, that he resolved to learn her to shoot too. They used to practice with pistols. Let her be ever so busy in her domestic duties, whether in the kitchen baking bread at which she had such a dainty hand, or at her ironing, or at her studies, raped

[sic] in a world of her own creating — it mattered not: if he called her to take a lesson, she would put it all down; his tender and affectionate 'Now my dear girl, let me see how well you can shoot to-day' was irristable to her filial nature . . . she would . . . take the pistol, which he had previously primed and loaded for her . . . with as firm a hand, and as steady an eye as any veteran of the camp, and fire.[33]

We will return to the deadly phallic load of Emily Brontë's highly 'penned' novel, in our analysis of *Wuthering Heights*. Here we can remark that, while it is necessary to restore the social history in which Emily Brontë's literary work developed, and legitimate to assert that, *in some sense*, her work provides a 'metaphor of the social struggle',[34] the traditional historicism of Marxist critics like Wilson and Arnold Kettle[35] tends to assume a textualizing, or 'metaphorizing', process that directly transfers coherent class-political positions to the text. This implies that the critic can do a one-to-one mapping of text to 'reality', or characters to classes. Thus, in *Wuthering Heights*, Wilson finds 'Heathcliff as representing the rebellious working men, and . . . Catherine . . . that part of the educated class which feels compelled to identify with their cause'.[36] Such a discourse tends to reproduce the 'expressive realist' assumption mentioned earlier, with the coherent 'truth/reality' that the reader recognizes through the transparent medium of the 'gifted' author's mind now invested with proto-socialist significance.

It is perhaps David Musselwhite's compact essay on *Wuthering Heights* as an 'unacceptable text', together with Francis Barker's response to the text's 'real conditions' — constituting a brief but highly suggestive exchange — that has raised the most cogent issues of textuality and ideology for a contemporary Marxist criticism; but unfortunately, this exchange is brief and prefatory.[37] Terry Eagleton's earlier chapter on Emily Brontë[38] remains the most complete recent Marxist analysis of *Wuthering Heights*. He understands the text's internal conflict between the 'social and the metaphysical' as a displaced working-out of ideological tensions associated with the encounter of different classes, with different class styles and projects — the 'brash vigour of the petty-bourgeois yeoman ... [and] the cultivating grace of the squirearchy'.[39] For Eagleton, *Wuthering Heights* confronts the radical difference of the positions that it fairly hurls against one another. The novel finally becomes an index of the impossibility of any secure ideological fusion, of any single 'world' that would integrate the values and interests of its constituent antagonists. Thus, Emily Brontë's work does not simply reflect existing ideological positions in, or transfer them to, the text, but produces an unprecedented 'ideological sub-ensemble'.[40] This new ideological position differs from those given by other producers of ideology working with the same raw materials (including in particular her sister Charlotte); it is a 'sub-ensemble' that is much less easily digestible within a developing literary tradition increasingly designed to support a dominant political and ideological *bloc*.

It is interesting that Eagleton's account renders almost invisible any sense in which Heathcliff textualizes images of the working class. Any such suggestion is subsumed within a discussion of the 'yeomanry', even when Eagleton refers directly to Wilson's article.[41] This is surely an over-compensation for Wilson's and Kettle's more simplistic, 'workerist' interpretations of the text, and, as such, part of a necessary enrichment of a highly overdetermined[42] image evoking many aspects of the dynamics of capitalist society, as will be suggested below. But one aspect of the capitalist dynamic, an aspect that a rural 'parsonist' ideology might be most likely to conflate with vaguer images of capitalism in general, is surely the spectre of the working class and its 'condition'. Even Gérin remarks:

In placing *Wuthering Heights* within the possibilities of its author's experience, it is of interest to remember, finally, that in August, 1845, Branwell was sent to

Liverpool ... It was the time when the first ship-
loads of Irish immigrants were landing at Liverpool
and dying in the cellars of the warehouses on the
quays. Their image, and especially those of the
children, were unforgettably depicted in the *Illustrated
London News* — starving scarecrows with a few rags
on them and an animal growth of black hair almost
obscuring their features. The relevance of such
happenings within a day's journey of Haworth ...
cannot be overlooked in explaining Emily's choice of
Liverpool for the scene of Mr. Earnshaw's encounter
with 'the gipsy brat' Heathcliff ... Emily left her
readers intentionally in doubt as to the origin of her
hero ... But who can say that he was not first given a
being and body by Branwell's report of starving im-
migrant children in the Liverpool streets? Branwell's
visit to Liverpool was in August 1845; the writing of
Wuthering Heights belongs to the autumn and winter
of that year.[43]

The point is not to ignore such raw material (as Gérin does
when she moves on to her analysis of this text that
supposedly 'has no concern for social questions'), nor to
take it as the explanatory 'reality' that the text more or
less precisely 'mirrors' (as Wilson tends to do), but to
indicate how it is transformed in the process of textualization, how its specific valence is written into the new,
peculiarly overdetermined signifying networks of the
literary text.

Eagleton's criticism focuses Marxism's attention on the
text as a site of ideological production, operating its own
specific transformations on the always-already-ideologized
'history' and 'reality' it takes up — a history and reality
that have always already been ideologically processed; but
his critical language is also heavily skewed towards an
analysis of what he calls the novel's 'ethical and ontological
idioms'.[44] Yet *Wuthering Heights*'s much-remarked transgressive power lies elsewhere, in the risks it takes with
psycho-sexual 'idioms' that threaten to destabilize the

subject's imaginary coherence. As Catherine Belsey remarks, ' "Identity", subjectivity, is . . . a matrix of subject-positions, which may be inconsistent or even in contradiction with one another.'[45] It is a virtual subject-position — or a set of partial, dispersed subject-positions — around which the text is organized and to which it appeals, that makes the literary text potentially captivating for its readers.[46] Traditional criticism implicitly recognizes this, and tries to abolish the disturbing proliferation of subject possibility by continually insisting on the perfect convergence of 'author-text-reader' in the 'really' literary text.

This active involvement in situating the subject helps to define literary practice as an ideological practice. For Althusserian theory, ideology has *'the function (which defines it) of "constituting" concrete individuals as subjects'*.[47] Ideology constitutes subjects by a process of 'interpellation', a kind of social 'hailing' or constitutive address through which individuals are called to recognize themselves spontaneously under certain names, within certain identities.[48] Ideology both works through language and textual discourse to give the subject positions from which to fix his or her relations to the real, and effaces the role of language in this construction of subjectivity. The power of ideology is not that it delivers to the rational subject a set of specifically political ideas, but that it offers to the psychological and linguistic subject a global, complexly articulated ' "lived" relation to the real'.[49] This is an active relation, in which the real and the imaginary constantly overdetermine each other, and through which the subject construes the social real in terms of his or her desire.[50] A complete analysis of the complex ideological effects of a literary text like *Wuthering Heights*, then, must certainly address the ways in which it revolutionizes, renews and/or restores the subject's imaginary identity, position and possibility within a disrupted sexual and social order.

It is recent feminist criticism that most energetically confronts questions of the text's interpellation of the

subject. Sandar Gilbert and Susan Gubar's chapter on
Emily Brontë[51] makes perhaps the strongest case for
Wuthering Heights as textualizing a kind of mythic revolution of gender identity against patriarchal definitions of
the self. Theirs is a complex study, which partly projects
Emily Brontë in a Bloomian agonistic struggle with Milton
as literary forefather,[52] and partly, with particular acuity,
reads the novel as a kind of anorexic nightmare of that
struggle. Their conclusion points to the 'autonomous and
androgynous (or, more accurately, gyandrous) whole' that
Catherine and Heathcliff constitute: 'a woman's man and
a woman *for herself* in Sartre's sense, making up one
complete woman'.[53] 'Gyandry', for Gilbert and Gubar,
means a kind of primal bisexual identity, dominated by
the feminine. Since they see Emily Brontë as one of
Milton's rebellious literary 'daughters', struggling with his
exclusive privileging of the masculine patriarch, this
gyandry, in their reading, folds in to a 'parodic, anti-
Miltonic myth' or 'an Original Mother' (Catherine
Earnshaw), who fragments into 'primordial selves' (the two
Cathys, Heathcliff and Hareton), and is finally 'redefined
as the patriarch's wife' (Cathy Linton, married to Hareton
Earnshaw).[54] Their argument also leans ambiguously
against Leo Bersani's careful post-Freudian reading of
Wuthering Heights as a, not pre-, but post-Oedipal experi-
ment in the subversion of identity.[55]

Its psychological complexity and theoretical-political
immediacy mark Gilbert and Gubar's as an argument that
addresses precisely those issues which contemporary
Marxism must also confront in the literary text in order to
develop a sufficiently comprehensive practice of ideological analysis. This book will accordingly maintain a
recurrent dialogue with Gilbert and Gubar's work as part
of its own attempt to understand, *within* an analysis of the
text's ideological management, the peculiar network of
psycho-sexual investments that initially scandalized her
critics and her sister, and have for so long given Emily
Brontë's work its 'strange power'.

1 Patriarchal Law and the Anarchy of Desire

There is no disputing the fact that *Wuthering Heights* has consistently evoked for its critical readers a strong sense of contradiction between two 'worlds' — opposed universes of symbolic activity, centred in the Heights and Thrushcross Grange. Critical attention usually focuses on Heathcliff as the character who provides the narrative energy that seems to power this mythic conflict. His ambivalently reciprocated love for Catherine registers as a problem of the order of a seismic fault, along which this imaginary universe tears asunder. A topic of somewhat calmer critical commentary has been the markedly heterogeneous effect of the text's language, its ability to evoke the most exact sense of 'realistic' detail alongside the most passionate sense of 'romantic' excess. Related to the complexity of the text's discourse is the complexity of its narration, its nested framing as a story the reader receives through a second-hand report of a report — passed through the first-person voices of two participant-observers.

This study will attempt to account for these textual 'problems' — the conflict between two 'worlds', the disruptive force of Heathcliff and Cathy's love, the discursive heterogeneity, and the complex narrational frame — as related aspects of what Fredric Jameson calls the text's 'libidinal apparatus'.[1] This term identifies a set of unconscious fears, desires and tensions that powers a narrative, and underlies the sympathy, suspense and identification it evokes. This is not exactly congruent with the author's or reader's 'own' unconscious structure of libidinal investments, because it is not something that exists 'before' the text; that would be another form of what we have identified as 'expressive realism'. It is rather a textual construct, through which an author's specific unconscious conflicts are pressed into the service of a dynamic narrative structure, where they are 'reinvested with new and unexpected content, and adapted to un-suspected ideological functions which return upon the older psychic material to re- or overdetermine it in its turn'.[2] The process of narrativization transforms what may have been a private fantasy, subjecting it to a multiplicity of new determinations, including those that derive from a social network of collective fears and desires. This over-determination thus constructs a communicable, publicly available fantasy, informed by a textual unconscious in which libidinal cathexes are displaced among the various elements of the narrative.

We can accurately extend the notion of 'libidinal apparatus' to 'ideological apparatus'. This textual un-conscious, public and historical, is a crucial element in the text's necessary ideological effect — which, again, is not the propagation of some explicit political doctrine, but the offer of an 'experience' through which social subjects can 'live' (without necessarily 'thinking about') appropriate class and sexual identities. At stake in the literary text is usually an 'imaginary resolution of real contradictions' deriving from a conflict of social forces, an unconscious libidinal conflict, *and* a conflict between psycho-sexual identity and social order. The literary text operates as an address to the subject, a discursive process that puts into play a matrix of explicit and implicit subject-positions, one of which will (or will not) tend to emerge 'spontaneously' as an imaginary site for the resolution of these conflicts, the site of an appropriately renewed 'lived relation to the real'.

In *Wuthering Heights*, the major tensions work themselves out on the imaginary terrain of the family. Heathcliff's entry, which sets the *story* in motion, is specifically
presented as disrupting not only the structure of a family,
but also a family structure — a carefully articulated order
of families within a self-contained social world. Mos⁺
narratives unfold from the disruption of an initial equilibrium; the ensuing narrative confusion becomes entwined
with a logical paradox and a libidinal contradiction, finally
driving towards a renewed, more complex, narrative
equilibrium that seems to resolve all these 'problems'.[3]
This is certainly the structural dynamic of *Wuthering
Heights*, a text where the constant scene of all this
narrative work is the family. The characters, the conflicts,
even the narrative structure of *Wuthering Heights*, are
staged in the family as a socio-economic institution, and
an arena of psycho-sexual struggle.

In this novel where entrances are very important, let us
begin by looking at the reader's entry into the narrative.
This is effected not by Heathcliff but by Lockwood, who
provides our only access to these virtual events, and who
arrives with the reader in the middle of the *story*. Our
entrance to the novel coincides with Lockwood's entrance
to Wuthering Heights, which is described in terms that
draw attention to significant socio-ideological and psycho-
sexual characteristics of the Heights and its inhabitants.
Lockwood's words mark the atmosphere of the Heights as
generally asocial and unsociable. Lockwood, who likes to
think of himself as aloof, is surprised to find that Heathcliff is even more unsociable. At first, Lockwood feels an
affinity with Heathcliff on the basis of this shared misanthropy, asserting that Heathcliff's 'reserve', like his
own, springs not from an 'underbred pride', but from an
'aversion to showy displays of feeling' (p. 7). And the little
private story which Lockwood confides to the reader,
about losing an eligible young woman because of this
'aversion', is not at all unlike the story of Heathcliff and
Cathy. Even Lockwood's remark that, 'By this curious

turn of disposition I have gained the reputation of deliberate heartlessness; how undeserved I alone can appreciate' (p. 7), anticipates Heathcliff's argument to Cathy after she marries Edgar.[4]

Lockwood, however, is a weak or even inverted analogue of Heathcliff, an 'antitype' whose function in the text is to register a difference from Heathcliff and to display much of what Heathcliff is not. Lockwood's elitist 'aversion' to feeling is, after all, very different from the lower-class shame and resentment that send Heathcliff away from Cathy. 'The fabrication of Lockwood', as one critic puts it, 'is the means by which *Wuthering Heights* speaks of its own textuality',[5] and rather than establishing Lockwood's narrative reliability, the text is here giving two implicit but important points of reference that can allow the reader to keep a distance from the 'lived relation to the real' which the text's narrative voice(s) will spontaneously offer. The first point of reference is that class sensibility differentiates otherwise similar characters, actions and discourses; the other is that 'our' narrator Lockwood — largely because of his particular class sensibility — has a symptomatic tendency to *misinterpret* what he sees and hears. For Wuthering Heights is a domain that is not only unsociable, in the sense of being isolated from a larger society; it is also internally asocial, enclosing an anarchic force that threatens to dissolve the cohesion of any 'world' (or 'self') the text might attempt to figure. While Lockwood is ultimately repulsed by the Heights, and cast back into a 'society' — 'the stirring atmosphere of the town!' (p. 368) — where he is more at home, Heathcliff's misanthropy turns out to signify something more acutely anti-social than mere 'reserve'.

It is with Lockwood's scene in Cathy's coffin-like, womb-like, bed that the text weaves a dense pattern of images of social dissolution overlaid with images of libidinal transgression. Cathy's diary, the first narrative that Lockwood passes on to us, establishes *the book* as an image whose ambivalence suggests the double-edged effects of culture and repression. On the one hand, Cathy's diary remarks, and is a mark of, the repression of youthful energy that she and Heathcliff suffer from books, especially from the servant and 'surly old man' Joseph, with his Old-Testament, patriarchal insistence that: 'they's good books eneugh if ye'll read 'em; sit ye dahn, and think uh yer sowls!' (p. 26). To which Cathy responds: 'I could not bear the employment. I took my dingy volume by the scroop, and hurled it into the dog kennel, vowing I hated a good book. Heathcliff kicked his to the same place.' But, for Cathy at least, the book has another function: her diary is itself a book, which she produces, and which remains for Lockwood — and for us — as a trace of the ambiguous power of her pen, of her capacity for channelling her rebellion and sublimating her desire, a capacity that Heathcliff certainly does not share:

> I reached this book, and a pot of ink from a shelf, and pushed the house-door ajar to give me light, and I have got the time on with writing for twenty minutes; but my companion is impatient and proposes that we should appropriate the dairy woman's cloak, and have a scamper on the moors, under its shelter. (p. 26)

If Cathy initiates rebellion by tossing Joseph's books into the kennel, Heathcliff carries it through by pulling her away from her own book — in the letter of the text, pulling her 'i' from sublimation ('diary') to her own sexuality ('dairy').[6] Thus, *Wuthering Heights* establishes the book as a complex image, the nexus of multiple associations linking cultural order and the control of language with sublimation and the self-control of desire;[7] and the text marks a difference in this regard between Cathy and Heathcliff, a difference that will pattern their relationship throughout the novel. Lockwood, of course, also writes his own diary (which we read), further enriching the complexity of the image by yoking the book and its associated sublimating impulse with the narrative function, an articulation that will also affect our understanding of Nelly Dean. That the semi-rebellious Cathy is more like the effete Lockwood in this respect than either is like the more radically disruptive Heathcliff also sets up literacy and sublimation as indicators of a class difference that tends, again, to dissociate otherwise similar characters.

The image of the book is as ambivalent as sublimation itself. If linguistic and cultural competence signifies repression, it also signifies a social power withheld from potentially troublesome classes, constantly kept on display and out of reach, somewhat like a shiny new gun. In *Wuthering Heights*, the word, as well as the pen, is 'not only mightier than the sword, but is also *like* the sword in its power.'[8] Thus, oppression is always associated with a clumsy silence, Heathcliff is found 'starving and houseless, and good as dumb, in the streets of Liverpool' (p. 45); Hindley enforces Heathcliff's illiteracy in order to exacerbate the difference between Heathcliff and Catherine; and Heathcliff, after seizing cultural and class power, attempts to deny literacy to Hareton. For the woman, the control of language and writing provides a kind of counter-phallic power which surreptitiously (and ironically) channels libidinal energies through social ambitions, whose ostensible pacifism and 'maturity' only mask a more subtle and effective form of unconscious aggression. This feminine linguistic and scriptural ability becomes especially important with Nelly Dean, whose ultimate narrative power in many ways parodies the authorial situation itself.

The first chapters of *Wuthering Heights*, then, quickly establish a remarkably rich discursive network in which each character becomes a node of conflicting forces that are specifically inflected in terms of social and libidinal energies. Heathcliff, who occupies one of the most heavily traversed character-positions, is invested with a rebellious energy that seems positive in its youthful, implicitly sexual form, but will turn dangerous in its adult guise as a principle of social violence (at least within the domestic society of the Heights). From the outset, the text seems at once fascinated with rebellion and worried that the disruption of the repressive mechanisms of culture will tend towards a mindless anarchy that would be unbearable in its own right. Lockwood's dream carries this ambivalent charge: we cannot help but sympathize with his revolt against the Reverend Branderham's stultifying sermon, but that revolt ultimately produces a situation where 'Every man's hand was against his neighbour' (p. 29).[9] Social 'misanthropy' leads to a state of confusion where 'every man's hand' can even be a child's wrist rubbed across a window pane:

> As it spoke, I discerned, obscurely, a child's face looking through the window — Terror made me cruel; and, finding it useless to attempt shaking the creature off, I pulled its wrist on the broken window pane, and rubbed it to and fro till the blood ran down and soaked the bed-clothes: still it wailed, 'Let me in!' and maintained its tenacious gripe, almost maddening me with fear. (p. 31)

The deliberate cruelty of Lockwood's response here is particularly striking, and yet it is symptomatic of much that will follow in *Wuthering Heights*. Indeed, a pervasive sadism saturates the novel's discourse. Critics have catalogued the violence, pain and torture — inflicted by cutting, stabbing or choking — that occur so much as a matter of course in the text as to become the very atmosphere of the narrative:[10] Cathy wakes Nelly by pulling her hair; while dining at the Lintons, Cathy shares her food with their dog Skulker, 'whose nose she pinched as she ate . . . kindling a spark of spirit in the vacant blue eyes of the Lintons'; Nelly describes a cold wind as 'a frosty air that cut about her shoulders as keen as a knife'; Isabella cries out 'as if witches were running hot needles through her'; the younger Cathy reacts to Hareton's touch as if 'he might have struck a knife into her neck'; the snow is 'suffocating' people; people are 'smothered in coats and furs', and so on.

All this sadism seems closely correlated with an infanticidal impulse: *sadism w/o subs*

> Without the care of their mothers, the children [in *Wuthering Heights*] find themselves in a fierce struggle for survival against actively hostile adults who seem obsessed with the desire to kill or maim them. From Lockwood's early dream of pulling the wrist of the ghost-child Catherine along a jagged window ledge, to Heathcliff's presiding with delight over the death of his overgrown child, the novel plays a multitude of insistent variations on the ghastly theme of infanticide.[11]

The sadistic, infanticidal violence of Lockwood the dreamer seems, again, to foreshadow Heathcliff's wideawake violence, from his torturing of animals to the following graphic, bloody tableau that recalls Lockwood's battle with the ghost-child:

> [H]e flung himself on Earnshaw's weapon and wrenched it from his grasp.
> The charge exploded, and the knife, in springing back, closed into its owner's wrist. Heathcliff pulled it away by main force, slitting up the flesh as it passed on, and thrust it dripping into his pocket. He then took a stone, struck down the division between two windows, and sprung in. His adversary had fallen senseless with excessive pain, and the flow of blood that gushed from an artery, or a large vein. (p. 218)

It is this kind of bloody scene that has provoked much Victorian and post-Victorian offence against the novel's 'excess of vividness', as 'either ... a symptom of immaturity, of insufficiently understood intensity, or as an error of judgement on the author's part'.[12] But it is the practice of the critic, not the 'mind of the author', that 'insufficiently understands' how the novel's complex intensity of affect might be directly related to the flow of blood — in cruel, even infanticidal, violence.

We can begin to understand this intensity when we understand that much of *Wuthering Heights*'s narrativizing work is done through what psychoanalytic theory calls the *displacement* of affect — the transfer of an emotional charge associated with one fantasy element on to an ostensibly different element which carries the charge awkwardly, 'so that the centre of the dream is shifted as it were, giving the dream a foreign appearance'.[13]

In Lockwood's dream, for example, a number of displacements are at work. One intense affect is certainly *fear*: 'terror' — 'The intense horror of nightmare' (p. 31) — makes Lockwood cruel and motivates his gruesome attack on the young spectre, a terror itself provoked by the child's attachment to him, from its desire to be 'let in'. But the object of fear in a nightmare is also an object of desire — an intense and taboo desire, which therefore evokes the fear of intense retribution. Thus, the sexual connotations of this young girl's apparition, her blood 'soaking the bedclothes', to a lonely, amorous young man who has been associated with Heathcliff suggest a taboo libidinal desire that functions as the repressed obverse of the sadism, infanticide and morbidity in *Wuthering Heights*.

To specify the dynamic of desire in question, we can now look again at Lockwood's dream to see how it puts into play more than the possession/dispossession of the social-phallic powers of the word and the pen. It also constitutes a remarkable discursive 'production' or 'staging' of a more primal scene of 'the father's seduction', a scene that in fact becomes the emblem and engine of this text's libidinal apparatus. Jane Gallop writes of how patriarchal law, in its disavowal of explicit sexual desire, only serves as the 'mask and support' of a more complex seduction.[14] Citing Luce Irigaray's book *Speculum* at one point, Gallop describes the dynamics of what Freud calls 'the typical Oedipus complex in women'.[15] Let's see what arises when we interrupt Jane Gallop's account of (Irigaray's reading

of) Freud's account of the father's/daughter's seduction
with Emily Brontë's account of Lockwood's encounter
with his succubus:

> The daugher's desire for the father is desperate:
> 'the only redemption of her value as a girl would be
> to seduce the father, to draw from him the mark if
> not the admission of some interest' (*Speculum*, p.
> 106). If the phallus is the standard of value, then the
> Father, possessor of the phallus, must desire the
> daughter in order to give her value. [... the hand
> clung to it, and a most melancholy voice sobbed, 'Let
> me in — let me in!' ... still it wailed, 'Let me in!' and
> maintained its tenacious gripe ...] But the Father is
> a man ... and cannot afford to desire otherness, an
> other sex, because that opens up his castration
> anxiety. ['The intense horror of nightmare came over
> me; I tried to draw back my arm, but the hand clung
> to it ... Terror made me cruel; and, finding it useless
> to attempt shaking the creature off, I pulled its wrists
> on to the broken pane, and rubbed it to and fro
> till the blood ran down and soaked the bed-clothes:
> still it wailed ... almost maddening me with fear.']
> The father's refusal to seduce the daughter, to be
> seduced by her ... gains him another kind of seduc-
> tion ... a veiled seduction in the form of the law ...
> The only way to seduce the father, to avoid scaring
> him away, is to please him, and to please him one
> must submit to his law which proscribes any sexual
> relation. ['How can I?' I said at length. 'Let *me* go,
> if you want me to let you in!' The fingers relaxed, I
> snatched mine through the hole, hurriedly piled the
> books up in a pyramid against it, and stopped my ears
> to exclude the lamentable prayer.] [16]

Lockwood's ambivalent gestures in this scene — first
forcibly penetrating ('knocking my knuckles through the
glass' (p. 30)) the membrane that separates male adult
from girl child, and then literally plugging 'the hole' with

words and writing, those marks of culture and the Law —
echo the Oedipal father's denial of his own seductive desire:

> '[I] t is not simply true . . . [nor] completely false, to
> claim that the little girl fantasizes being seduced by
> the father, because it is just as pertinent to admit that
> *the father seduces his daughter* but that, refusing to
> recognize and realize his desire — not always it is true
> —, *he legislates to defend himself from it*' . . . The
> father's law is a counterphobic mechanism. He must
> protect himself from his desire for the daughter.[17]

Here again, Lockwood functions as a displaced and parodic
version of Heathcliff, who immediately takes Lockwood's
place in the bedchamber with an unambiguous, unafraid
overture of the self and appeal to the other: 'He got on the
bed, and wrenched open the lattice, bursting, as he pulled
at it, into an uncontrollable passion of tears. "Come in!
come in!" he sobbed. "Cathy, do come. Oh do — *once*
more!" ' (p. 35).

Lockwood and Heathcliff, then, register different,
tendentially opposing, versions of the same Oedipal desire,
a contradictory drive that will dominate the scene of this
text as it dominates the scene of the bedchamber. The
reader finds the first marks of this desire at the entrance to
the text, especially in the images that adorn 'Mr Heathcliff's
dwelling' (p. 4). Lockwood follows Heathcliff through a
threshold attended by 'A wilderness of crumbling griffins
and shameless little boys', which, under the inscription of
the ancestral patriarch, 'Hareton Earnshaw', and the date
'1500' (p. 5), suggests the primitive, youthful phallic
fertility of family origins. The 'range of gaunt thorns all
stretching their limbs one way, as if craving alms of the
sun' suggests, on the other hand, a dessicated, sterile sexual
tension of the 'dry man in a dry land' genre, if not, in the
'craving of the sun', some kind of fixation with, or sub-
servience to, the maternal.

This is, therefore, a highly wrought textual threshold: an
architectural portal which momentarily freezes Lockwood

and Heathcliff within a common frame before their
entrance to the 'atmospheric tumult' of Wuthering Heights;
an entrance to the narrative — occurring on the third page
of the text, and to the narration — emphasizing as it does
Lockwood's ushering of the reader simultaneously into the
text, the Heights and Heathcliff's presence. And it is a
passage to the innermost imaginary recesses of Emily
Brontë's text, a passage under the *penates* whose penes are
exposed into what Lockwood calls the 'penetralium', the
'family setting-room', known metonymically — or 'pre-
eminently', according to the text — as 'the house' (p. 5).[18]
This threshold marks the house itself, invested with the
Name and power of the Father, as a kind of ultimate
signifier of the Earnshaw family. It marks the family as the
site of a mythic-historic libidinal tumult, and it establishes
the 'pen-' as an uncannily fertile textual seme.

Still other textual traces establish Heathcliff as the agent
of an Oedipal project. We never read exactly why Mr
Earnshaw decided to bring Heathcliff across this threshold,
but once Heathcliff has penetrated the 'innermost recesses'
of the family estate, very strong textual ties are established
between Heathcliff and the father. Earnshaw, who 'took to
Heathcliff strangely' (p. 50), names him after, and treats
him as, a son — more in the father's favour than either of
his natural offspring; he even comes to see the treatment
of Heathcliff as a test of his paternal authority. As Nelly
Dean remarks:

A nothing vexed him [Earnshaw], and suspected
slights of his authority nearly threw him into fits.
   This was especially to be remarked if anyone ever
attempted to impose upon, or domineer over, his
favourite: he was painfully jealous lest a word
be spoken amiss to him, seeming to have got into his
head the notion that, because he liked Heathcliff, all
hated, and longed to do him an ill-turn. (p. 50)

Certain 'accidental' characteristics of their names

further strengthen the text's identification of Heathcliff
with the 'old master'. Heathcliff's name of course is a kind
of semiotic twin of 'Wuthering Heights', the name of the
Earnshaw estate, and he and Earnshaw are the only major
characters referred to by respective half names, with the
former's first (and very un-Christian) name completing the
latter's 'family' name, further emphasizing their semiotic
complementarity. Thus, 'Heathcliff', 'Heights' and 'Earnshaw' become so textually affiliated as to form virtually a
single signifying unit, with 'hero' (protagonist), 'house/
family' and 'father' as interchangeable signifieds. As one
critic has aptly remarked, Heathcliff 'is more an Earnshaw
than the Earnshaws themselves'.[19]

The thematic and scriptural congruence between Heathcliff and the father, along with the phallic, patriarchal
images surrounding Heathcliff at the threshold of the
narrative, and the complex of desire and fear imaged in
Lockwood's — the mock-Heathcliff's — dream, form a key
network of textual markers. They insistently suggest the
Oedipal significance of the disruption which Earnshaw
produces in his family with the introduction of Heathcliff,
the disequilibrium to which the narrative is subjected
under the Name of the Father, and the transgressive feel of
the desperate, frantic and deadly attraction between
Heathcliff and Cathy. In the symbolic order of this text,
Heathcliff is more than a foster-brother, more even than a
disguised blood-brother of Cathy: he is a displaced father,
whose entrance into the Earnshaw family opens a 'mythic',
contradictory and disruptive version of 'the father's seduction'.[20] Heathcliff is identified with the father (both the
'real' and the mythic primal father), enters into a
tempestuous, passionate and 'taboo' relationship with the
daughter, and seeks to become 'master' over the son. The
'cosmic' and 'elemental' quality of Heathcliff and
Catherine's love is one prominent formal sublimation of
this incestuous desire which powers the fiction. The
curious complex of infantile/infanticidal fear and sadism,
which first appears in Lockwood's dream, provides a

'counterphobic' energy, a denial of, or overcompensation for, the incestuous desire.

In one evocative tableau, Cathy's body becomes an ana-clitic link in the signifying chain of displacement between the father and Heathcliff:[21] 'Miss Cathy had been sick, and that made her still; she leant against her father's knee, and Heathcliff was lying on the floor with his head in her lap' (p. 53). This tableau is itself embedded in a series of ambivalent gestures that register the 'antithetical sense' of the primal seductive scene.[22] Here, Cathy is between paternal reprimands as she is between Heathcliff and the father. She has just been 'repulsed' by her father, in the most severe terms of patriarchal judgement: 'I cannot love thee . . . ask God's pardon . . . my mother and I must rue that we ever reared thee!' (p. 52), and is about to be reprimanded by him again: 'Why canst thou not always be a good lass, Cathy?' (p. 53). Her response to the father's last question is rhetorically and ontologically devastating: 'Why cannot you always be a good man, father?' she says, and then kisses his hand and sings him to 'sleep' — that is, death (p. 53).

Cathy's 'in-betweeness' here is an emblem of the place she comes to occupy in the narrative dynamic. In-between love and hate for the father — in-between, that is, two forms of the father's demand — the young Cathy acts decisively (if, textually speaking, unconsciously) to resolve her situation: she replaces the father with the father's other, the patriarchal, upright father who condemns with the phallic, infantile father who responds.[23] In one sense this decisiveness makes her, as the tableau suggests, the father's momentary analogue, in the same authoritative relation to Heathcliff as the father is to her. But the older Cathy, under the different pressure of a choice about marriage, will be resituated in-between Heathcliff and Edgar — within a transformed version of the father's double demand. At this later stage, she will not be able to respond to her own satisfaction, and will have no retort to Heathcliff's reprimand, which will now be devastating to her.

Heathcliff finally emerges as a primary agent of narrative activity. A displacement of the Oedipal father, he becomes an intensely overdetermined textual figure, defining a position in the text where many associations cross and overlap. He is associated with youth, with phallic and paternal authority, with the Earnshaw family and the Heights; and he is associated too with lower-class *ressentiment*, and with the disruption of social (especially marital and familial) order and of cultural impediments to gratification. Each of the elements that converge on this character-site is itself 'antithetically' inflected, a bearer of severe, often contradictory, pressures. For example, Heathcliff's energy is associated with youth, but youth is itself associated with the past as imaged in Heathcliff and Cathy's childhood; the past, in turn, is associated with the patriarchal origins of the Earnshaw family. If Heathcliff's energy is a displaced representation of Earnshaw patriarchal power, his infantile libidinal licence, displayed in his utter disrespect for the conventional ways of managing desire, none the less threatens to disrupt patriarchal Law. If his energy is masculine and phallic, it finds a feminine complement, if not analogue, in Cathy. And as with Cathy, Heathcliff's relation to his own desire is modified by the changing, contradictory pressures of the narrative situation.

This complexity is not the result of some aesthetic confusion or 'excess', but a necessary aspect of Heathcliff's function as a primary agent of the narrative work, of what we have called the text's libidinal/ideological apparatus. Within this structure, Heathcliff is the nodal point for a set of forces that are driving the text towards a specific imaginary resolution of its conflicted subject-positions – a resolution that can fix a centre of intelligibility, and forcibly and finally stabilize a process of textualization that is constantly destabilized by incompatible demands. Indeed, the power of *Wuthering Heights* derives in large part from the unmediated clash of incompatible totalitarian demands for narrative resolution, as well as the intrinsic instability of that resolution – dominated by what we can now call the anarchy of desire — which Heathcliff tends to impose on the textual dynamic. For there is a counter-tendency in *Wuthering Heights*, another overdetermined site on which a complex of forces gather to hurl themselves into the textual fray, steering the narrative towards an opposed, equally totalitarian resolution. This position, this alternate project for the text and for the subject, is also affiliated with the narrative tasks of a specific character, a less insistent but no less persistent and pervasive presence — the narrator herself, Nelly Dean.

2 The Phallic Mother and the Sadism of Control

Nelly Dean is as important a character as Heathcliff in *Wuthering Heights*, and in a crucial sense his true and effective antagonist.[1] The structure and significance of *Wuthering Heights* is not centred on a presence — 'Heathcliff', or even 'Heathcliff and Cathy' — but is destabilized around an absence, a space 'in-between' across which Cathy becomes increasingly dispersed, and at the poles of which Heathcliff and Nelly become tendentially situated, like the foci of an ellipse.

Like any other fiction, *Wuthering Heights* generates not real but virtual human subjects and historical events, unfolding within the illusory coherence of a virtual time and space — what is sometimes called the narrative *diegesis*.[2] And, as in many other fictions, certain characters seem to be given a voice that more directly controls how the reader, as well as the characters, 'lives' this virtual 'reality'. The 'reader' is, after all, a virtual construct — the subject addressed as s/he who accepts this diegetic space. As a principal character, or virtual subject of the narrative, Nelly has an active, even directive, role in the unfolding events; as the principal[3] narrator — a still-virtual narrating subject whose voice should not be confused with the voice of the text — she controls Lockwood's, and through him the virtual (naive) reader's, 'lived' diegetic experience of the text. To take Nelly as 'benevolent' and 'wholesomely nurturing', as 'detached' from a story that she tells 'without herself becoming ensnared in it', is to take for granted the very assumption on which she works in order to 'cook' the narrative so as to render herself invisible to Lockwood and the reader, and is to miss some of the more complex and disturbing implications of her narrative situation as 'general mother', 'patriarchy's paradigmatic housekeeper', 'charged with the task of policing the realm [she] represent[s] '.[4]

To understand how this text develops it is necessary to situate Nelly, and her narrative power, *inside* it, and to establish our own critical distance from her voice. It is curious how Nelly's presence as one 'I' of the text seems not to deprive her (for most readers) of any of the authority that would be invested in the more impersonal 'objectivity' of an 'omniscient' narrative voice. To the contrary, making her 'I' explicit actually encourages the reader to identify with the familiar kind of 'objectivity' that seems to inhere in her 'common sense', in a way that helps to render invisible her own interested activity in the narrative. It is important to 'see' Nelly's activity in this text not so much to understand the non-existent 'mind' of another character, but in order to resist the offer of a narrative ego that Nelly's voice carries — an ego that presents itself as this text's 'natural' ground for the most conventional fixation on 'characters'. As a virtual subject like any other character within the narrative dynamic, Nelly Dean cannot really 'know' what she is doing in this text; but the reader cannot know how this text functions without understanding the sense in which it presents her, no less than it does any other character, as if she *'thinks' that she does*.

Like, and in opposition to, Heathcliff, Nelly emerges as a primary narrative agent, who puts into motion a complex of social and psychological tendencies that are mediated by, but finally independent of, her 'intentions'. As the narrative unfolds, the stakes in this centrifugal tension become clearer, but an antagonism is visible even in the

beginning of Nelly's narration when Heathcliff is intro-
duced into the Heights. Nelly clearly feels that she is at the
centre of the family circle that Heathcliff invades, as she
indicates with an offhand emphasis in her opening description of 'the old master's' departure for Liverpool: 'my
mother had nursed Mr. Hindley Earnshaw . . . and I got
used to playing with the children — I ran errands too'; 'he
turned to Hindley, and Cathy, and me — for I sat eating
my porridge with them'; 'He did not forget me . . . He
promised to bring me a pocketful of apples and pears'
(pp. 43–4).

Earnshaw, of course, returns with a 'dirty, ragged, black-
haired child' (p. 44), and Nelly doesn't fail to emphasize
Cathy and Hindley's disappointment at getting a foster-
brother instead of the presents they had been promised.
Nelly neglects to mention whether she was disappointed
over the forgotten fruit, but it is not difficult to read her
reaction to the 'stupid little thing' between the lines of the
following account:

> They [Cathy and Hindley] entirely refused to have
> it [Heathcliff] in bed with them, or even in their
> room, and I had no more sense, so I put it on the
> landing of the stairs, hoping it might be gone on the
> morrow. By chance, or else attracted by hearing his
> voice, it crept to Mr. Earnshaw's door, and there he
> found it on quitting his chamber. Inquiries were made
> as to how it got there; I was obliged to confess, and in
> recompense for my cowardice and inhumanity was
> sent out of the house.
>
> This was Heathcliff's first introduction to the family.
> On coming back a few days afterwards, for I did not
> consider my banishment perpetual, I found they had
> christened him 'Heathcliff:' it was the name of a son
> who had died in childhood. (p. 46)

This incident exemplifies Nelly Dean's *style*, as both
narrator and participant. In the first sentence, Nelly admits
her complicity in turning out Heathcliff, but in a way that

makes her seem less responsible for the affair than Hindley and Cathy: though she was herself 'hoping' for Heathcliff's disappearance, it was only because she 'had no more sense' that she gave in to her companion's insistence. Her 'confession' to Earnshaw, which seems not to include such extenuations, she treats with mock seriousness. Then, the same Nelly who did not have the 'sense' to resist the children of the household becomes sensible enough to take it upon herself to reinterpret the terms of the father's punishment. Heathcliff's acceptance as a son within the Heights-Earnshaw circle occasions Nelly's temporary banishment — a portent of a later exile that Nelly will accept only under much more favourable terms. Heathcliff's entrance into the family thus disrupts an equilibrium, and catalyses the mitosis of a previously unified family cell: 'Miss Cathy and he were now very thick; but Hindley hated him, and to say the truth I did the same.'[5] This incident can be seen as the first instance in this text of what Roland Barthes calls a cardinal function in the narrative,[6] a point where the narrative irreversibly shifts gears, taking up one potential path of development, and closing off others.

Nelly certainly values her place in the Earnshaw family, and is capable of asserting what in her mind seems more the status of a 'foster sister'[7] than a servant ('I ran errands *too*'); she is jealous and contemptuous of the newcomer ('it') who intrudes in that situation, and she acts with considerable independence and cunning to protect her position. Throughout the novel, one comes up against Nelly's unobtrusive, 'common sense' insistence on a quite specific interpretation of events — an interpretation designed, I shall argue, to efface her own active role in defending certain imaginary values and advancing certain imaginary interests. Like Heathcliff, Nelly is assigned a precarious narrative project that sometimes poses contradictory demands. Her narrative control is opportunistic and self-effacing, an 'invisible hand' to whose manipulations Lockwood, and by extension the reader, must, and are usually pleased to, submit. If Heathcliff catalyses forces in *Wuthering Heights* that tend towards an anarchic social and libidinal violence, Nelly Dean, for her part, imposes on the discourse and the narrative of the text an implacable sadism of control.

Heathcliff and Nelly Dean share an analogous 'foster' relation to the Earnshaw family — in it, but not of it. As Gilbert and Gubar comment, 'like Heathcliff, Nelly seems to have been a sort of stepchild at the Heights.'[8] For some time, especially under Hindley's rule at the Heights, they share a common predicament determined by their class. Hindley treats Heathcliff as an upstart rival and seeks to 'reduce him to his rightful place' whenever possible, by driving a wedge of class distinction between him and Cathy. Hindley encourages the Lintons' refinement of Cathy with their 'fine clothes and flattery' (p. 65) finishing technique, and he exacerbates Heathcliff's class insecurity by forcing him to lose 'the benefit of his early education'; as Nelly says, 'continual hard work, begun soon and concluded late, had extinguished any curiosity he once possessed in pursuit of knowledge, and any love for books or learning. His childhood sense of superiority, instilled into him by the favours of old Mr. Earnshaw, was faded away' (p. 84).

Nelly's sympathy with Heathcliff here is based in part on their common position as servants or household workers. It is not quite, as Gilbert and Gubar suggest, that 'Nelly is excluded from the family, specifically by being defined as a servant', while Heathcliff is not — with Nelly therefore, 'Luckily for her . . . avoid[ing] the incestuous/egalitarian relationship with Hindley that Catherine has with Heathcliff'.[9] Heathcliff and Nelly are both put in their place as servants — by different 'masters', at different times, for different reasons, with the most striking variation in treatment being that between the original Mr Earnshaw and Hindley. And if Nelly is 'ineligible for marriage into either family' (p. 290), so also is the young Heathcliff;[10] otherwise, Cathy would not marry Linton, and the story would end. Gilbert and Gubar seem at times to have a peculiar understanding of the condition, if not the psychology, of the servant. It is a curious reckoning, for example, by which Nelly is 'lucky' to have 'avoided' any egalitarian relationship within her masters' family. (We see below Nelly's considerable nostalgia for just such a relationship.) And Nelly seems invisible to Gilbert and Gubar precisely *as* a servant, when they assert that Hindley's marriage 'installs an adult woman in the small family circle for the first time since the death of Mrs. Earnshaw' (p. 267). Nelly is twenty (the same age as her foster-brother and new 'master', Hindley) at this point, and perceives Frances, who treats Cathy like a 'sister' (p. 56), as 'rather young' (p. 55). Nine months later, Nelly is 'adult' enough to begin nursing the newborn Hareton.

Again, however, despite Heathcliff and Nelly's analogous positions in the household, differences begin to over-shadow seeming similarities. The Nelly-Hindley associ-ation, for example, |still holds. Although Nelly finds Hindley's domain 'an infernal house' (p. 81), she retains her special feeling for Hindley as a 'foster-brother'; she and Joseph are the only two servants who can 'bear his tyrannical and evil conduct' in the Heights after Frances's death (p. 81). Nelly is so undisturbed by Hindley's antics and the phallicism of this text's diegetic space, that she reacts with complete — one might say cutting — sang-froid to Hindley's threat to make her swallow a carving knife: 'He held the knife in his hand, and pushed its point between my teeth: but, for my part, I was never much afraid of his vagaries. I spat out, and affirmed it tasted detestably — I would not take it on any account' (pp. 91–2). Nelly's tie to Hindley is even more strongly evoked by an uncharacteristic lyrical meditation that occurs later in the text, one of the few passages of Nelly's discourse that does not contain some sadistic metaphor:

The sun shone yellow on its [the guide stone's] grey head, reminding me of summer; and I cannot say

why, but all at once, a gush of child's sensations
flowed into my heart. Hindley and I held it a favourite
spot twenty years before.

I gazed at the weather-worn block; and, stooping
down, perceived a hole near the bottom still full of
snail shells and pebbles which we were fond of storing
there with more perishable things — and, as fresh as
reality, it appeared that I beheld my early playmate
seated on the withered turf, his dark, square head
bent forward, and his little hand scooping out the
earth with a piece of slate. (p. 133)

It does indeed seem, as Gilbert and Gubar remark,[11]
that Nelly was once as close to Hindley as Catherine was to
Heathcliff; it seems, that is, that she occupies a crucial role
in the text's chain of (Oedipal) displacements, repetitions
and inversions — 'little hands' and all.

Perhaps even more important for distinguishing Nelly
and Heathcliff are the different functions — the 'field-hand'
versus the 'house servant' — that they perform within their
shared position as members of a dominated class. These
different kinds of work often give rise to divergent ideological identifications with the 'master's' interests,
tending to channel ambition and resentment in contradictory directions. The conflict in the novel between 'outdoor' and 'indoor' concerns registers, among other things,
this difference between 'appropriately' illiterate and im-
miserating labour in the fields and more intellectually
subtle and ambitious labour in the book-lined rooms:

[Hindley] deprived [Heathcliff] of the instructions
of the curate, and insisted that he should labour out
of doors instead, compelling him to do as hard as any
other lad on the farm. (p. 56)

I have undergone sharp discipline, which has taught
me wisdom; and then, I have read more than you
would fancy, Mr. Lockwood. You could not open a
book in this library that I have not looked into, and
got something out of also. (p. 78)

Even Nelly's attempt to mollify Heathcliff's class insecurity in relation to Edgar is framed in terms of an
ambitious self-projection in the image of one's betters, a
strategy for pacifying class rage in order to achieve an
imaginary promotion conceived as more secure and more
important than actual social empowerment:

> 'I wish I had light hair and a fair skin, and was dressed
> and behaved as well, and had a chance of being as rich
> as he will be!'
>
> 'And cried for momma, at every turn — . . . Oh,
> Heathcliff, you are showing a poor spirit! Come to
> the glass and I'll let you see what you should wish . . .
> Wish and learn to smooth away the surly wrinkles, to
> raise your lids frankly, and change the fiends [eyes]
> to confident, innocent angels, suspecting and doubting
> nothing, and always seeing friends where they are not
> sure of foes. Don't get the expression of a vicious cur
> that appears to know the kicks it gets are its desert,
> and yet hates all the world, as well as the kicker, for
> what it suffers.'
>
> 'In other words, I must wish for Edgar Linton's
> great blue eyes, and even forehead', he replied. 'I do
> — and that won't help me to them.'
>
> 'A good heart will help you to a bonny face, my
> lad . . . who knows, but your father was Emperor of
> China, and your mother an Indian queen. . . . Were I
> in your place, I would frame high notions of my
> birth; and the thoughts of what I was should give me
> courage and dignity to support the oppressions of a
> little farmer!' (pp. 71–2)

As a servant in Hindley's household, Nelly is of course
precisely 'in Heathcliff's place', and the combination of
dissembling naivety backed by supreme egotism which she
suggests to Heathcliff is a fair projection of her own
strategy for social promotion. But any envy of, or aspira-
tion for, the 'fine clothes and flattery' world of the
Lintons is completely alien to Heathcliff's fierce pride,

which is more attuned to the turbulent traditions of the Earnshaw family. The text marks Heathcliff's inability to stomach any kind of submissive, integrationist strategy when, immediately after the above conversation with Nelly, he throws a tureen of hot applesauce in Edgar Linton's face.

Thus, although they begin as 'foster' siblings in a similar predicament, Heathcliff and Nelly quickly diverge into very different kinds of foster figures, pulling in opposite directions in this family romance. If the letter of the text quickly inscribes Heathcliff as an implicit imaginary substitution for the Father, the narrative promptly propels Nelly into explicit action as 'foster-mother', even 'general mother';[12] but this role does not unequivocally imply that Nelly is 'benevolent . . . a nurse, a nurturer'.[13] In the textual unconscious, Nelly functions in the much more complex role of what Jane Gallop calls the 'phallic mother', the mother who situates herself in, and speaks for (in the voice of), the Father's Law:

> [I]t is more usual and more comfortable to associate the phallic with the Father. . . . The assumption that the 'phallus' is male expects that the exclusion of males be sufficient to make a non-phallic space. The threat represented by the mother to this feminine idyll might be understood through the notion that Mother, though female, is none the less phallic . . . The inability to separate the daughter, the woman, from the mother then becomes the structural impossibility of evading the Phallus.
>
> According to Kristeva the Primitive Father is 'more obvious than the phallic mother and, in that sense, less dangerous'. . . . If the phallus 'can only play its role when veiled' (Lacan), then the phallic mother is more phallic precisely by being less obvious.[14]

Nelly is the female figure who wields the phallic tools of the symbolic order,[15] of language and culture, and works to prohibit the consummation of the father's desire.

In so doing, she becomes an agent of patriarchal Law, the 'counterphobic mechanism' that is the 'mask and support' of the father's incestuous desire/demand. It is the violence of this Law that underlies Nelly's control of the text. Despite Nelly's projection of herself in the role of benevolent, protective mother, trying to shield the innocent children from the destructive fury of the raging father-figure (personified alternately by Hindley and Heathcliff), the subdued sadism of her phallic-maternal control is symptomatically present in her own crucial interventions in this narrative, as well as in the constant stream of tortuous metaphors that run through *her* discourse like hot needles through a woman's body. Thus, in the complex 'antithetical' inflections of each of these figures, Nelly is in one sense, as an agent of the Law, more phallic than Heathcliff.

The function of the 'phallic mother' is also implicit in Lockwood's dream. Is not the rather dandyish Lockwood's sawing of the child's wrist on the jagged window pane a more sustained and deliberate torture than any of the 'demonic' Heathcliff's arbitrary, impetuous cruelties? The womb-like environment of the bedchamber, whose orifice Lockwood plugs with the paraphernalia of the Word, is his refuge against the appeal of the child-spectre, and he is ruthless in preventing her intrusion. Lockwood's refusal of this opening images the Oedipal father's refusal of sexual otherness, a refusal to sever the narcissistic attachment to the phallic mother:

> [I] f the father desires his daughter as daughter he will be outside his Oedipal desire for his mother, which is to say also 'beyond the phallic phase'. So the law of the father protects him and patriarchy from the potential havoc of the daughter's desirability. Were she recognized as desirable in her specificity as daughter . . . there would be a second sexual economy besides the one between 'phallic little boy' and 'phallic mother'. An economy in which the stake

might not be a reflection of the phallus, the phallus's desire for itself.[16]

Of course, if Lockwood's chamber is womb-like it is also tomb-like, a site of oceanic absorption and deadly equilibrium. This aspect of the phallic mother reappears, on the one hand, in the 'open' and 'outdoor' sense of Heathcliff and Cathy's relationship, which threatens to tear open this enclosure, and, on the other hand, in Nelly's concern for closing the windows of the text's houses, and presiding over the caskets of its dead. The primal scene in the bed-chamber, the womb-tomb-library, resumes in the library where Nelly pleases Lockwood with the story of this book, a repetition of all books — an open and shut case.

Edgar too, despite his weak and effete appearance, because of his 'uprightness', and not 'despite' but *because* of his 'superegoistic qualities', wields more effectively than Heathcliff 'the power of the patriarch'. As Gilbert and Gubar recognize, this power 'begins with words'; it is a mastery 'contained in books, wills, testaments, leases, titles, rent-rolls, documents, languages, all the paraphernalia by which patriarchal culture is transmitted'.[17] But this is also the paraphernalia of which Nelly knows 'more than you would fancy', and in the novel it is Nelly who most shrewdly and effectively wields the power of words. After all, at stake here (in this text and this 'paraphernalia') is not just patriarchal but also *class* culture, and Edgar's secure position in the latter gives his words the power to make dependent bodies appear, in order to compensate for his own physical weakness and threaten Heathcliff. It is because Nelly does not have the same, and seeks some, security within class culture, because her power begins and *ends* with words, that she must make even shrewder use of their effects.

Nelly's way with words resumes in another sense the function of the 'phallic Mother'. Nelly not only tells a story to Lockwood, she constantly *listens* to Cathy's story — or more precisely, to Cathy's attempts to get her own life/story straight. Nelly's quite active and 'directive' listening, as we shall see in some detail below, helps keep Cathy confused about what she wants and what she 'is'. Nelly's oral, interlocutory relation to Cathy evokes an increasingly troubling transference.[18] If anything, this relation parodically inverts the 'nourishing' relation of mother to daughter, just as the phallic mother's oral relation to the daughter, which 'ought to be one in which the daughter absorbs (from) the mother . . . is confused with the mother's absorbing the daughter':

> When the daughter begs 'Keep yourself/me also outside', the statement presupposes that the mother controls the process of absorption, of differentiation and identity. In Lacanian terms, the silent interlocutor, the second person who never assumes the first person pronoun, is the subject presumed to know, the object of transference, and the phallic Mother, in command of the mysterious processes of life, death, meaning and identity.[19]

While the patriarchal power of the Law and Word is judiciously wielded by magistrate (Edgar) and narrator (Nelly), Heathcliff's blatant enactment of the Primitive Father's uncompromising desire becomes its embarrassment, the revelation of its precarious sexual body. This more explicit eroticization paradoxically helps to evoke the perception that, 'on a deeper associative level, Heathcliff is "female" . . . what Elaine Showalter calls "a woman's man".'[20] In a quite peculiar sense, in Gallop's terms, Heathcliff figures less as 'phallocentric' than as 'phallo-eccentric':

> Or, in more pointed language, he is a prick . . . [T]he prick is 'beyond good and evil', 'beyond the phallus'. Phallocentrism . . . [is] an upright matter. The prick, in some crazy way, is feminine.
>   . . . The prick, which as male organ might be expected to epitomize masculinity, lays bare its

desire. Since the phallic order demands that the law rather than desire issue from the phallic position, an exposure of the father as desiring, a view of the father as prick, a view of the father's prick, feminizes him . . . The phallic role demands impassivity; the prick obviously gets pleasure from his cruelty. The evidence of the pleasure undermines the rigid authority of the paternal position.

. . . If the Name-of-the-Father is phallocentric law, then the father's prick is the derision of his Name.[21]

In this reading, then, all these characters become less figures in the successful constitution of an idyllic androgynous or 'gyandrous' whole, than actors in an imaginary cycle of Oedipal release and repetition. Emily Brontë's text may 'unveil the obscene privilege of the phallus',[22] but still seems held within the structural impossibility of its evasion. The 'germ of a terrible dis-ease with patriarchy'[23] that Heathcliff introduces into this text is the disease of the Father's desire, of the daughter's seduction, itself. And this text's virtual author is truly, wherever she turns, 'raped(t) in a world of her own creating'.

3 The Contradictory Articulation of the Narrative

It is in the passage between the Primitive Father's phallic desire (of which Heathcliff becomes the surrogate) and the upright father's patriarchal Law (of which Edgar becomes the surrogate), a passage mediated by the 'phallic mother' (of which Nelly Dean becomes the surrogate), that Cathy's self dissolves, and that she succumbs to the suicidal anorexia that Gilbert and Gubar analyse so well.[1] Cathy's inability to constitute a stable self or self-image, an inability that makes her finally a character more acted upon than acting, is the acute symptom of the daughter's paralysis in the double-bind of the Oedipal seduction's contradictory demands. As Gilbert and Gubar argue, along with Leo Bersani, the instability of the ego may at times be part of a liberating, (gy)androgynous eroticism in *Wuthering Heights*. But the novel is certainly equivocal in this respect: there is a recognition that such instability has more destructive effects once Cathy is 'simultaneously catapulted into adult female sexuality *and* castrated'.[2] Post-Oedipal trauma is usually a tragic-ironic analogue of pre-Oedipal 'androgyny'. If Cathy's adult madness is a rebellion, it is — exactly like a 'hunger strike'[3] — a sign of that most desperate situation in which destroying one's self seems the only way of attaining the recognition of the other.

There are other things at work in this tug of war that

tears Cathy apart. Cathy may be the object of struggle in the narrative, but as such she also functions as a surrogate — for the Earnshaw family itself. At stake here is not Cathy's mental health, or her (or woman's) 'autonomy', but the fate of the family. The 'personal' plights of Cathy, Nelly and Heathcliff only have narrative significance in relation to the structural changes taking place in the family; it is the problematic of the family that determines, and sporadically changes, the relative importance of each character and each character's 'concerns'.

The scene in which Cathy confesses her feelings about Edgar and Heathcliff to Nelly, with Heathcliff overhearing just enough to drive him away, subtly positions Nelly and Heathcliff at the poles of Cathy's 'in-betweeness', while serving as another cardinal function or narrative hinge on which the text turns in a specific direction. This hinge turns, as it were, on Nelly's deliberate passivity, and on what I have called her directive listening. In her silence, Nelly controls the crucial piece of information in this scene, the knowledge of Heathcliff's presence, and this gives her decisive power within the communicative structure of the scene. She allows certain elements of Cathy's enunciation to be overheard by Heathcliff, and allows him to slip away without hearing others; she deflects or minimizes some elements of Cathy's enunciation, and amplifies and reflects others back to Cathy. All this is done in a way that effectively encourages a specific action on the part of a Cathy who, now faced with a decision about a husband rather than a playmate, does not know how to make up her own mind. The communicative structure of this scene is in many respects analogous to the structure of the narrating situation itself: Nelly, the 'subject presumed to know', controls — with her silence as much as her words — what Heathcliff hears (and what Cathy sees) in this scene, just as she controls what Lockwood hears (and the reader sees) in the story. In both cases she works implicitly to encourage certain attitudes, if not actions.

The communicative stucture of this scene is also not

incidentally analogous to the structure of the 'directive listening' situation between analyst and analysand. Gallop notes Freud's discovery that psychoanalysis only works through *transference*, the analysand's transfer of a previous libidinal attachment on to the analyst, and Gallop further emphasizes the 'decisive structural relation' of the figure of the governess, maid or nurse, to the analytic situation:

> Later Freud will theorize that all relations to others merely repeat the child's original relation to the mother, the first other. Transference is not peculiar to psychoanalysis, but is actually the structure of all love. Even the relation to the father . . . is already actually a transference of mother-love onto the father. What distinguishes psychoanalysis from other relations is the possibility of analyzing the transference, of being aware of the emotions as a repetition, as inappropriate to context . . . What facilitates the recognition of the feeling as transference, as an inappropriate repetition, is the fact that the analyst is paid. The money proves that the analyst is only a stand-in. Rather than having the power of life and death like the mother has over the infant, the analyst is financially dependent on the patient. But, in that case, the original 'analyst', the earliest person paid to replace the mother is that frequent character in Freud's histories, the nursemaid/governess.[4]

Thus, Gallop can say that 'Psychoanalysis can be and ought to be the place of symbolic inscription of the governess.'[5] And Nelly Dean functions in this sense as a rather conservative kind of analyst who, through directive listening rather than overt advice, helps Cathy to orient herself towards the 'adult', sublimated sexuality that is congruent with submission to the father's Law — that is, to marriage with Edgar Linton. Cathy addresses Nelly as 'the subject presumed to know'.

'Sublimation' is certainly an apt category for understanding Cathy's choice between Edgar and Heathcliff, which she imagines as a choice between 'heaven' and 'hell' (pp. 99–100), between 'the foliage in the woods' and the 'eternal rocks beneath' (p. 101). The 'catechism' that Nelly 'put[s Cathy] through' (p. 97) evokes the problematic of sublimated versus direct libidinal satisfaction, of the substitute versus the primary love-object. Nelly, however, stubbornly avoids *recognizing* the problem that this little Socratic exchange *produces*. At the outset of the discussion, Nelly establishes the 'principle' of Cathy's dilemma – a principle that she refuses to modify – in terms of upholding the Word as Law: 'You have pledged your word, and cannot retract' (p. 96). When Cathy persists in demanding to be told 'whether I'm right' (p. 98), Nelly's response seems to open a doubt:

> Perfectly right; if people be right to marry only for the present. And now, let us hear what you are unhappy about. Your brother will be pleased . . . The old lady and gentleman will not object, I think – you will escape from a disorderly, comfortless home into a wealthy respectable one; and you love Edgar, and Edgar loves you. All seems smooth and easy – where is the obstacle? (p. 68)

Yet the irony in the first sentence of this quote is not in Nelly's voice but in the text's. Such irony is one mark of the difference between Nelly's voice and the text's, and of Nelly's role as an implicated character-narrator, not the implied author. For Nelly refuses Cathy's necessary response: ' "*Here*! and *here*!" . . . striking one hand on her forehead, and the other on her breast. "In whichever place the soul lives – in my soul and in my heart, I'm convinced I'm wrong!" ', with an abrupt, and stubbornly naive: 'That's very strange! I cannot make it out' (p. 98). When Cathy tries to explain through the account of a dream (the classical psychoanalytic situation), Nelly, who is 'superstitious about dreams' (p. 99), insists: 'I won't hear it, I won't hear it!'; and Cathy actually has to hold Nelly down to recount her dream of the divorce of heaven and hell:

> heaven did not seem to be my home; and I broke my heart with weeping to come back to earth; and the angels were so angry that they flung me out, into the middle of the heath on the top of Wuthering Heights; where I woke sobbing for joy. ... I've no more business to marry Edgar Linton than I have to be in heaven; and if the wicked man in there had not brought Heathcliff so low, I shouldn't have thought of it. It would degrade me to marry Heathcliff, now; so he shall never know how I love him; and that, not because he's handsome, Nelly, but because he's more myself than I am. Whatever our souls are made of, his and mine are the same, and Linton's is as different as a moonbeam from lightning, or frost from fire. (pp. 99–100)

Nelly's reluctance to listen to Cathy's dream is complemented by her unwillingness to speak up to prevent Heathcliff's flight. Nelly's silence constitutes the crucial moment in Cathy's speech, when Nelly allows Heathcliff to slip away at the precise moment that 'he heard Catherine say it would degrade her to marry him' (p. 100). Nelly's silence here is not passive but *active*; in order to confirm its effect, she must quickly invent a lie in response to Cathy's query about the stirring behind her: ' "Joseph is here," I answered, catching, opportunely, the roll of his cartwheels up the road' (p. 100).[6]

Nelly's rejection of Cathy's imaginary identification with Heathcliff ('Nelly, I *am* Heathcliff' (p. 102)) reveals a sharp, and increasing, textual differentiation between Nelly's project and the desire which constitutes Heathcliff and Cathy's love. It also marks a growing identification of Nelly with the Linton alternative — that is, with the libidinally conservative, and socially shrewd, management of desire.

On the one hand, Nelly thus enacts a 'progressive'

quasi-analytic project of tearing Cathy out of the Imaginary – that is, out of an attachment to the desiring Father (itself, as we have seen, a transference of the attachment to the enveloping Mother). This incestuous obsession with the Father *is* in the realm of morbidity, closure and self-absorption/consumption, the realm of the pre-Oedipal and the pre-linguistic, of the womb and the tomb:

> if all else perished, and *he* remained, I should still continue to be; and if all else remained and he were annihilated, the Universe would turn to a mighty stranger. I should not seem a part of it ... Nelly I *am* Heathcliff – he's always in my mind – not as a pleasure, any more than I am always a pleasure to myself – but, as my own being – so, don't talk of our separation again – (pp. 101–2)

On the other hand, Nelly works to pull Cathy out of an Imaginary self-annihilation in the heat of the Father's phallic desire, only to pull her into a Symbolic order whose potentially liberating linguistic power is recuperated for another kind of morbidity and closure under the cold hand of the dead Father's Law:[7] ' "If I can make any sense of your nonsense, Miss," I said, "it only goes to convince me that you are ignorant of the duties you undertake in marrying; or else, that you are a wicked, unprincipled girl"' (p. 102). The womb and the tomb reappear in the library. But the project of this text, in which Cathy is a token of the Earnshaw family, is not finally to subsume the Earnshaws within the Lintons, but quite the reverse.

This soliloquy once again, this time in Cathy's own voice, clearly and explicitly overlays the psycho-sexual problematic with class and social concerns. It is only because Hindley has 'brought Heathcliff so low', making marriage to him a 'degrading' prospect, that Cathy even 'thinks of' taking the path of instinctual repression implied in a marriage to Edgar Linton. In fact, she imagines such a marriage as part of an entire life's project and strategy, determined by Heathcliff's class predicament, and designed

to help him (somewhat more concretely than Nelly's
admonition to 'frame high notions of [his] birth') escape
the 'oppressions' of farmers who wield the power of
property: 'Every Linton on the face of the earth might
melt into nothing, before I could consent to forsake Heathcliff. Oh, that's not what I intend . . . Nelly . . . did it
never strike you that if Heathcliff and I married, we should
be beggars? whereas, if I marry Linton, I can aid Heathcliff
to rise, and place him out of my brother's power' (p 101).

Nelly's rejection of Cathy's plan ('that's the worst
motive you've given' (p. 101)) ignores its affinity with
Nelly's own little creed as expressed to Lockwood: 'Well,
we *must* be for ourselves in the long run; the mild and
generous are only more justly selfish than the domineering . . .' (p. 114). Nelly's increasing identification with
the Linton alternative may be determined less by 'principle'
than by her strategy — much like that she urged on Heathcliff — of gradual advancement through an overtly placid
but aggressively opportunistic acceptance of a subordinate
class position. Nelly knows, after all, that a marriage to
Edgar would mean for her, as well as for Cathy, an 'escape
from a disorderly, comfortless home into a wealthy,
respectable one'. But if it is ostensibly too 'unprincipled'
for Nelly, Cathy's strategy, in both its economic and
libidinal registers, is far too indirect for Heathcliff. His
desire will not stand down before the marriage banns, and
his independence will be won without, and indeed against,
any favours from the rural petty-aristocracy, let alone
those that might issue from Cathy's dependence on Edgar
Linton. Thus, Heathcliff's impulsive flight at just the
wrong (right) moment in Cathy's plaint is a symptomatic
'accident', determined by the sullen class resentment that
shapes his character. The insecurity that underlies his
silence and self-effacement in this scene contrasts with the
discursive control of Nelly, apparent in her deliberate,
considered, withholding of the utterance that could have
prevented his extended departure.

But Heathcliff does leave, and Nelly, perhaps justifying

her selfishness as of 'the mild and generous' sort, eventually 'lay[s] the blame of his disappearance' on Cathy, 'where indeed it belonged, as she well knew' (p. 109). Cathy contracts a fever waiting overnight in the rain for Heathcliff to return, and after a rather gruesome treatment at the Heights that lets even more blood flow ('[the doctor] bled her, and he told me to let her live on whey and water gruel ... I cannot say I made a gentle nurse, and Joseph and the master were no better' (p. 109)), Cathy finishes her convalescence at Thrushcross Grange. There, she fatally infects Mr and Mrs Linton with this disease that results from her excessive desire for Heathcliff. With Heathcliff gone, Cathy is smoothly married off to Edgar, and Hindley is delighted to see her 'bring honour to the family by an alliance with the Lintons' (p. 110). Nelly is 'persuaded', after holding out for 'munificent wages' (p. 110), to go along as Cathy's protector and companion in the move to the 'wealthy, respectable' world of the Grange. Heathcliff moves in quite the opposite direction, and reappears only when he can be master of the Heights in its most anarchic and disreputable condition, when it is most sharply focused as the opposite of all that the Grange represents.

The confession scene is, thus, a point of no return in the narrative, and from this point the text intensifies the antagonism between Heathcliff and Nelly. In so far as Heathcliff is associated with a primitive sexual-social energy, Nelly becomes increasingly associated with a sophisticated sexual-social moderation. Heathcliff enacts both the primal Father's incestuous desire and an oppressed class's resentful vengeance. Nelly enacts the phallic Mother's defence of the Law against incestuous desire, and a class project orientated towards moderate upward mobility within accepted parameters of class domination. She takes up her new place in the Linton family and the Grange, a more elevated position in the social hierarchy,[8] and she becomes linked to established culture and social equilibrium in various forms (harmonious family life, gradual fulfilment of rising expectations, dissimulation of desire and ambition rather than protest, resistance or rebellion). Like Heathcliff, Nelly condenses and catalyses a totalizing complex of forces, steering the narrative towards a resolution on its own terms. This direction is towards the repression and effeteness of a rich but decadent social and cultural life, as figured in the 'heavenly' Linton household that Cathy and Heathcliff mock through the window of Thrushcross Grange — as figured even in the vacant blue eyes and pallid countenance of Edgar Linton, which Nelly encourages Heathcliff to take as his own imaginary reflection, but which Heathcliff himself defiles with hot food from the Earnshaw kitchen.

Cathy is the stake — or, more precisely, the token of what is at stake — in this tension between Heathcliff's and Nelly's implicit projects. The tension originated in Heathcliff's disruptive arrival under the father's cover, precipitating Nelly's immediate attempt to get rid of him, and her subsequent temporary banishment; it centres on Heathcliff's and Nelly's respective claims as representatives, *in loco parentis*, of the Earnshaw family's 'fate' — its interests, its posterity, its future. Heathcliff, who comes to occupy and control the family estate, and obsessively pursues the daughter, forcibly returns to the family the repressed 'phallo-eccentric' libidinal energy of the Primal Father, as first figured in the 'crumbling griffins and shameless little boys' on the façade of Wuthering Heights. This energy shatters the stifling domination of a congealed patriarchal Law, but also threatens the family's final, anarchic dissolution. Nelly Dean, who moves to the Grange, guides the family with subtle, quasi-maternal care towards a cultural integration and progressive social advancement in the image and place of the Lintons. With this advancement, she seeks to ensure the family's survival (and coincidentally her own self-interest), while threatening to extinguish, with the veiled phallic power of Word and Law, the libidinal energy that is the Earnshaws' 'difference'.

Nelly's maternal 'interest' in the Earnshaw family is

more obvious in her assumption of a protective role towards Cathy in the move to the Grange, and in her parallel reluctance to give up her influence on Hareton, whom she describes as 'the last of the ancient Earnshaw stock' (p. 79), and whom she 'had just begun to teach ... his letters' (p. 110); as one of the servants told Nelly when Hareton was born: 'it will be all yours when there is no missis!' (p. 79). Later, this maternal role is re-emphasized in young Cathy Linton's lament to Nelly: 'What shall I do when *papa and you* leave me? ... How life will be changed ... when papa and you are dead' (p. 281, my emphasis). But Heathcliff's own intervention on behalf of the Earnshaw family is dramatically figured in his inadvertent 'salvation' (p. 93) of Hareton, when Hindley carelessly drops the child Nelly calls 'the little wretch' (p. 93) from the top of the stairs: 'Heathcliff arrived underneath just at the critical moment; by a natural impulse, he arrested [Hareton's] descent, and [set] him on his feet' (p. 93).

This last incident emphasizes that the 'projects' in question are objective narrative tasks, imperfectly related to any character's illusory subjectivity or intention. Heathcliff's rescue of 'the last of the ancient Earnshaw stock' is an 'accident' forced by narrative determinations; he suffers 'the greatest anguish at having made himself the instrument of thwarting his own revenge' (p. 93). As we shall see, the 'antithetical' character of Heathcliff's and Nelly's roles in the text will make each into an ironic 'instrument' of an outcome that she or he seeks most determinedly to prevent, an outcome that represents the other's partial success.

4 The Daughter's Division

It is their double articulation, their definition in terms of both social and libidinal tensions, that gives Nelly and Heathcliff — and the textual dynamic itself — their peculiar ambivalence. If the text is dominated by the effects specific to a particularly intense Oedipal (family) romance, the outcome of this romance is itself determined by the demands of a social project in which the family is implicated. Nor is this social project some 'extrinsic' intrusion in a text whose Oedipal tropes and effects, as we have described them, seem clearly those of a neo-Gothic romance. The novel, in fact, carefully inscribes such a social articulation in its specific mode of 'staging' the romance, and in so doing figures the *necessary*, *internal* 'opening' of the Oedipal drama. For the family cell that serves as the crucible of libidinal anxiety and the object of psychoanalysis is not a hermetic entity, disconnected from the social organism that in fact sustains it.

As Gallop points out, the idealist notion of the autonomous family unit that underlies 'the pernicious apoliticism'[1] of conservative psychoanalysis is undermined by the constant irruption of society and class into the practice of psychoanalysis itself: 'The family never was, in any of Freud's texts, completely closed off from questions of economic class. And the most insistent locus of that intrusion into the family circle ... is the maid/governess/nurse. As Cixous says, "she is the hole in the social cell".'[2]

The taboo against incest is in fact the obverse of a demand for endogamy *within* a larger social frame, an injunction to marry within a somewhat wider social 'family' defined by class. The social intruder — in but not of the family or its social circle — provides the most persistent threat of displaced 'exogamous' incest:

> If sexual relations are understood as some kind of contact with alterity . . . then the incest taboo would institute a prohibition against alterity within the family circle, a law ensuring the 'imaginary' closure of the cell . . . Lévi-Strauss finds that the correlate to the incest taboo is endogamy. Sexual relations are with someone whose alterity is limited within the confines of a larger circle. Exogamy, marrying outside the larger circle, is equally a violation of the incest taboo. Marriage outside of class or race might represent a contact with a non-assimilable alterity, thus like actual incest bringing unmitigated heterogeneity within the family circle.[3]

Although Gallop is thinking here exclusively of the 'governess' figure as social intruder and potential seducer, *Wuthering Heights* obviously splits these functions and makes them more complex. It is the servant or household worker, the paid intruder, whether male or female, that makes for a 'hole in the cell', a point of contact between family and social world that threatens the family's imaginary sense of integrity. Heathcliff is the seducer and prime usurper in this textual context, and is doubly incestuous as an imaginary Oedipal father *and* a 'real' class-exogamous 'gipsy'. But Nelly, too, is constantly scolded for overstepping the limits of her 'place', and operates within and upon the family with a managerial ambition as insistent as Heathcliff's libidinal drive. She also operates a kind of discursive seduction on Lockwood, and through him, on the reader. The family's fate ultimately rests on the text arranging a precarious economy of limited transgression through which each of these characters both enables and deflects the project of the other. The point remains that class and social questions are crucial to the text's narrative dynamic because they are *intrinsic* to its figuration of the Oedipal romance that grounds whatever melodramatic effect we might discern.

Indeed, part of *Wuthering Heights*'s peculiarity as a 'romantic' text is its inclusion of a discursive antithesis to romance. Thus, many critics have seen the novel as a kind of generic oxymoron, where a precise social 'naturalism' lives in untroubled adjacency to the typically spectacular flashes of the Gothic. This generic paradox may be symptomatic of a narrative on the edge, as it were, of romance and realism — a romantic narrative that testifies to the increasing impossibility of romance. This generic tension is itself refracted through the tendential opposition between Heathcliff and Nelly, which structures the text's libidinalideological apparatus. What could be a more appropriate index of the potential for a subversive Romanticism to fold itself into the secure drama of bourgeois order than this text in which an archetypal 'Byronic' figure of romantic rebellion can only be spoken as a *parole* in the *langue* of a crafty manager of household affairs, 'patriarchy's paradigmatic housekeeper'?[4]

The pressure of socio-ideological forces on the Earnshaw family romance becomes more acute after Cathy's marriage to Edgar, the decline of the Heights under Hindley, and Heathcliff's reappearance as a wealthy 'gentleman'. Even after Nelly moves to the Grange and smoothly transfers her fealty to her new Linton 'master', she seeks to maintain her influence on the fate of the Earnshaw family. Nelly is particularly upset, after Heathcliff's return, by his renewed contact with Cathy:

> My heart invariably cleaved to the master's [Linton's], in preference to Catherine's side; with reason, I imagined, for he was kind, and trustful and honourable: and she — she could not be called the *opposite*, yet ... I had little faith in her principles, and still

less sympathy for her feelings. I wanted something to
happen which might have the effect of freeing both
Wuthering Heights and the Grange of Mr. Heathcliff,
quietly, leaving us as we had been prior to his advent.
His visits were a continual nightmare to me; and, I
suspected, to my master also. His abode at the Heights
was an oppression past explaining. (p. 132)

Nelly fears Heathcliff's disruption of the social and
libidinal order into which Cathy has been integrated *at
the Grange*. She is satisfied with the 'Linton-izing' of
Cathy's youthful sexual energy, and apprehensive that the
circuit of desire between Cathy and Heathcliff will be re-
activated as a result of Cathy's untrustworthy 'principles'.
But to prefer the situation (as Nelly also did when she put
Heathcliff on the stair) 'prior to [Heathcliff's] advent' is
also to prefer the ascendancy of the Lintons. The weak,
auto-destructive decline of the Heights under Hindley
was tolerable to Nelly, and would eventually have resulted
in her/Linton's custody of Hareton, the Earnshaw heir.
Under Heathcliff, this process is transformed into an in-
tolerably *aggressive* corruption of socio-libidinal Law and
order, visiting itself even upon the Grange, and threatening
to prevent the final peaceful assimilation of the Earnshaw
family therein. Nelly's firm and explicit alliance with
Edgar Linton, in opposition to Cathy and Heathcliff,
indicates at this point the extent to which she has become
'more of a Linton than the Lintons themselves'.

Thus, although he seems securely settled at the Heights,
when Heathcliff embraces Isabella, Nelly seizes the oppor-
tunity to foment a crisis that might result in his ejection
from the Grange. First, she indignantly calls Cathy's
attention to Heathcliff's 'making love' to Isabella. Cathy
at first reacts with righteous class propriety, telling Nelly:
'To hear you, people might think *you* were the mistress!
You want setting down in your right place!' (p. 137). But
Nelly's provocation of Cathy's jealousy does precipitate
an argument between Cathy and Heathcliff, and Nelly,

after 'the conversation ceased', goes off to 'seek the master' to inform him of the 'scene in the court . . . and the whole subsequent dispute' (p. 139). There follows Edgar's embarrassing confrontation with Heathcliff, where Cathy prevents Nelly fetching any help for Edgar and locks the four of them (Nelly and Linton, and Heathcliff and Cathy) in the room, berating Edgar in a tone 'implying both carelessness and contempt' (p. 140). The scene ends with Edgar, 'overcome' with 'mingled anguish and humiliation' (p. 141), desperately attacking Heathcliff, then running for help while Heathcliff 'smashes' (p. 142) the door open with a poker.

Having precipitated two arguments and exacerbated the antagonism between Edgar and Heathcliff that will be fatal for Cathy, Nelly, 'anxious to keep her [Cathy] in ignorance' (p. 142), is called on by a distraught Cathy, 'who did not know my [Nelly's] share in contributing to the disturbance' (p. 142), to assume the expected role of 'nurturing' confidant:

> Nelly, say to Edgar, if you see him again to-night, that I'm in danger of being seriously ill . . . What possessed him to turn listener? Heathcliff's talk was outrageous, after you left us; but I could soon have diverted him from Isabella, and the rest meant nothing. Now, all is dashed wrong by the fool's-craving to hear evil of self that haunts some people like a demon! Had Edgar never gathered our conversation, he would never have been the worse for it . . . To this point he has been discreet in dreading to provoke me; you must represent the peril of quitting that policy, and remind him of my passionate temper, verging, when kindled, on frenzy — I wish you could dismiss that apathy out of your countenance, and look rather more anxious about me! (p. 143)

Nelly's silence here is again active and constitutive, implicitly but deliberately 'keeping Cathy in her ignorance' by affirming Cathy's misapprehension that it was Edgar who eavesdropped on her argument with Heathcliff after they thought Nelly had left the room. A more careful audience than Lockwood would compare Cathy's 'after you left us' with Nelly's earlier claim that she had remained in the kitchen until 'the conversation ceased'. A critical reader will also recognize that the text has continually constructed Nelly as someone likely to realize that Edgar would not have been hurt by what he had not 'gathered'. But then, too, Heathcliff would not have been driven from the Grange, 'leaving us as we had been'.

Dismissing Cathy's concerns, Nelly tells Edgar nothing of Cathy's real or pretended illness. Nelly claims to believe, with some initial justification since Cathy had expressed a desire to 'frighten' Edgar, that Cathy only wants to 'multiply his annoyances for the purpose of serving her selfishness' (p. 144). But Cathy wants to 'frighten' Edgar in order to keep him *away* from her and avoid another 'annoying' scene: 'he might come and begin a string of abuse, or complainings; I'm certain I should recriminate, and God knows where we should end!' (p. 143). And when Edgar does visit Cathy, after Nelly says nothing as she meets him 'coming towards the parlour' (p. 144), Cathy's actual condition seems so poor that Nelly has to persuade him, *without fully believing it herself*, that Cathy is just pouting:

Mr. Linton stood looking at her in sudden compunction and fear. He told me to fetch some water. She had no breath for speaking.

I brought a glass full: and, as she would not drink, I sprinkled it on her face. In a few seconds she stretched herself out stiff, and turned up her eyes, while her cheeks, at once blanched and livid, assumed the aspect of death.

Linton looked terrified.

'There is nothing in the world the matter', I whispered. I did not want him to yield, *though I could not help being afraid in my heart*.

'She has blood on her lips!' he said, shuddering,

> 'Never mind!' I answered tartly. And I told him how
> she had resolved, previous to his coming, on exhibiting
> a fit of frenzy. (p. 145, my emphasis)

The 'nurturing' Nelly seems rather ungenerous to her
charge, and, acting 'the mistress' again, virtually commands
Edgar to ignore Cathy's condition. Cathy goes on her
'hunger strike', and Nelly — again despite her own 'alarm'
(p. 149) — 'keep[s Edgar] ignorant' (p. 155) of Cathy's
worsening condition, telling Lockwood with perhaps ironic
justification that 'the Grange had but one sensible soul in
its walls, and that lodged in my body' (p. 147). Edgar, in
the meantime, shuts himself up in the library, 'continually
among his books, since he has no other society', a fact that
prompts Cathy to exclaim: 'Among his books! . . . And I
dying! I on the brink of the grave! . . . Are you speaking
the truth about him now! Take care. Is he actually so
indifferent for my life? . . . What in the name of all that
feels, has he to do with *books*, when I am dying?'

In railing against Edgar's bookish indifference, Cathy
seems unaware that it is Nelly's determinate silence that
allows Edgar to remain isolated in his library, that comforting womb of words. Thus, Cathy at first pleads with
Nelly in these tones: 'Cannot you inform him that it is
frightful earnest? . . . Cannot you tell him I will [die of
hunger]? . . . persuade him — speak of your own mind —
say you are certain I will!' (p. 148). But Cathy also begins
to see Nelly in a different light: 'Shake your head as you
will, Nelly, *you* have helped to unsettle me!' (p. 153).
Furthermore, Cathy explicitly associates what she perceives
as Nelly's antipathy for her with the regime of the Lintons —
the upright, lifeless people of the Grange, who would
prefer the peace of Cathy's righteous death to the household havoc of her 'unprincipled' desire:

> I begin to fancy you don't like me . . . and they have
> all turned to enemies in a few hours. *They* have,
> I'm positive; the people *here*. How dreary to meet
> death surrounded by their cold faces! . . . And Edgar

standing solemnly by to see it over; then offering prayers of thanks to God for restoring peace to his house, and going back to his *books*! (p. 149)

At one point in her 'delerium', Cathy evokes a striking image of Nelly as a sterile figure whose 'pretended' maternal concern is designed to enable a kind of nightmare sadism: 'I see in you, Nelly . . . an aged woman — you have grey hair, and bent shoulders. This bed is the fairy cave under Peniston Crag, and you are gathering elf-bolts to hurt our heifers; pretending, while I'm near, that they are only locks of wool' (p. 150).[5] It does not unduly strain this novel's discourse to read the 'cave under Peniston Crag' as a teasing textual figure of the maternal phallic — the womb under the domination of the tablet of patriarchal law — and as a repetition of that curious secret cache, under the stone — a 'rough sand-pillar' (p. 133), cut with the letters of this text — that marks the junction between the Heights, the Grange and the village, where Nelly hid the shells and pebbles that are the tokens of her playful idylls with Hindley. But 'Peniston(e)'[6] can be broken up in other ways, which we will discuss below, that mark it as an even denser textual palimpsest.

When Edgar finally sees Cathy's condition and realizes Nelly's part in concealing it, the ensuing exchange confirms Nelly's role as an overzealous agent of the Linton regime, and leads Cathy emphatically to reaffirm her perception of Nelly's pseudo-maternal function:

'I desire no further advice from you', answered Mr. Linton. 'You knew your mistress's nature, and you encouraged me to harass her. And not to give one hint of how she has been these three days! It was heartless!' . . .

I began to defend myself, thinking it too hard to be blamed for another's waywardness!

'I knew Mrs. Linton's nature to be headstrong and domineering', cried I; 'but I didn't know that, to humour her, I should wink at Mr. Heathcliff. I per-

formed the duty of a faithful servant in telling you,
and I have got a faithful servant's wages! Well, it will
teach me to be careful next time. Next time you may
gather intelligence for yourself!' . . .

Confused as Catherine was, her wits were alert at
applying our conversation.

'Ah! Nelly has played traitor,' she exclaimed,
passionately. 'Nelly is my hidden enemy — you witch!
So you do seek elf-bolts to hurt us!' (p. 157)

Nelly's response here is less an explanation of why she
neglected to inform Linton of Cathy's condition than a
defence of her own 'intelligence' activities, which she clearly
understands as an integral aspect of 'policing the realm she
represents'.[7] It is just this conversation, revealing her role
as informer, that Nelly was trying to prevent in keeping
Edgar away from Cathy, and it is Cathy's recognition of
Nelly's 'intelligence' role that prompts Cathy to confirm
the feeling that Nelly had been her 'hidden enemy' all
along. It is Nelly who intervenes between Cathy and Heathcliff at the most crucial moments: she does her best to
redirect Cathy's 'unprincipled', taboo attraction to
Heathcliff towards more respectable fixations; she provokes
Heathcliff's expulsion from Cathy's company after he
returns; and she sits quiet, allowing Cathy to be overcome
by 'the aspect of death'.

Nelly, then, is also *Heathcliff's* 'hidden enemy', continually involved in the crises that force his separation
from his love-object. And in so far as his quest for Cathy
is an aspect of the unconscious textual project associated
with the Earnshaw family, Nelly's thwarting of that desire
eventually becomes a kind of betrayal of her ostensibly
protective maternal function in the family romance. Thus
she comes to maintain her charge, the Earnshaw daughter,
in what feels like an imprisonment within the Linton
domain, and even seems willing to sacrifice Cathy, as well
as Heathcliff, to preserve the sterile Linton regime of
family Law and order, and her own position within it.

With Heathcliff's return, the mature Cathy — now implicated in the magisterial networks of marriage, spousehood and family respectability — is thrown into renewed conflict over her reawakened desire for him. At this stage of the text's spiral of repetitions, however, the social stake is much higher. Cathy's suicidal impulse is certainly a symptomatic response to what has thus become a more desperate and claustrophobic in-betweeness and indecision — between submission to the upright father's law and participation in the desiring father's forbidden seduction, between loyalty to Linton and attraction to Heathcliff. But Cathy's self-destruction also portends the effective self-extinction of the Earnshaw family, which seems to be a necessary correlate to its elevation and integration, under Nelly's guardianship, into the 'wealthy, respectable world' of the Lintons.

Nelly's response to Edgar, once her deceit is discovered, is also an address to her primary and secondary audiences, Lockwood and the reader, and a textual testing of the reader's relation to the narrative voice. For her 'I began to defend myself, thinking it too bad to be blamed for another's waywardness!' can only be accepted at face value by an audience, like Lockwood, which is seduced by the false intimacy of the narrative ego. When Nelly says, '"I knew Mrs. Linton's nature . . ." cried I', it is the textual 'I' which is also crying for sympathy — pleading for its audiences' continued acceptance of its invisibility, of its lack of specific, antagonistic and agonistic, performance. This is a sympathy that the critical reader must be more reluctant than Lockwood to give.

5 The Limits of the Textual Ideology

Whatever the designs of its characters, *Wuthering Heights* is not interested in abolishing, but in preserving and advancing the Earnshaw 'difference' — the phallo-eccentric eroticism of direct Oedipal desire; the text is also interested in ensuring the social survival of this desire, if only in a modulated form. This textual 'interest' coincides with the *double* paradox of the Oedipal seduction: if the phallus has its lasting victory in the imposition of patriarchal Law in the form of the incest taboo, the 'passage' of that Law itself depends on the consummation (some'where', if only in the unconscious) of the Oedipal crime that the Law is designed as much to *punish* as to prevent. Thus, in *Wuthering Heights* the tendentially contrary projects enacted by Heathcliff and Nelly veer towards complementarity, as characteriological 'intentions' are deflected by narrative compulsions.

A key example of such deflection is the textual *turn* — another cardinal function or narrative gear-change — represented by Heathcliff's final, passionate encounter with Cathy. This encounter is made possible by a contradiction that arises between the libidinal and social axes of Nelly's pseudo-maternal role: a contradiction between the 'task' of resisting Heathcliff's incestuous/exogamous seduction of Cathy, and the task of looking after (and coincidentally conflating) the Earnshaw family's *and* her own 'best interests in the long run' — that is, securing their possibilities of progressive social advancement. Nelly's dilemma arises when Heathcliff, in his undaunted quest for revenge, outflanks Nelly by marrying Isabella — a union whose potentially disturbing ramifications Nelly specifies quite clearly in her complaint about the Linton father's insufficiently patrilineal testament: 'I mentally abused old Linton for — what was only natural partiality — the securing his estate to his own daughter, instead of his son's' (p. 201).

Heathcliff's marriage to Isabella, combined with the ailing Cathy's precarious pregnancy,[1] diminishes the chances of the Linton property 'being secured from a stranger's gripe by the birth of an heir' (p. 165). In fact, Nelly gets a vivid glimpse of Heathcliff's strategy when she visits the Heights, and Isabella says: 'he says he has married me on purpose to obtain power over [Edgar] . . . The single pleasure I can imagine is to die, or to see him dead!' (p. 185). Heathcliff's reply confirms the point:

> There — that will do for the present!. . . If you are called upon in a court of law, you'll remember her language, Nelly! And take a good look at that countenance — she's near the point which would suit me. No, you're not fit to be your own guardian, Isabella, now; and I, being your legal protector, must retain you in my custody, however distasteful the obligation may be. (p. 185)

Thus, there is a new, considerable stake in maintaining good relations with Heathcliff, when Nelly, despite her understanding of the 'cruelty and selfishness of [Heathcliff's] destroying Mrs. Linton's tranquillity for his satisfaction' (p. 186) — and indeed her understanding that 'Another encounter between you [Heathcliff] and the master will kill her altogether!' (p. 181) — agrees, or is 'forced to agree' (p. 187), to become Heathcliff's 'intelligence' agent (p. 187) and arrange a clandestine rendezvous between him and Cathy. The Nelly who had been Linton's 'faithful servant' and the text's guardian against transgression, not willing to 'wink at' Heathcliff's presence at the Grange, now becomes the accomplice of Heathcliff's desire, 'playing that treacherous part in my employer's house' (p. 186). Although she half-heartedly rationalizes her agreement with Heathcliff by hoping (in contradiction to the danger she correctly foresaw in the remark quoted above) that the encounter 'might create a favourable crisis in Catherine's mental illness' (p. 188), her more succinct and ironically open explanation seems rather closer to the mark: 'it was wrong, though expedient' (p. 188).

The beginning of a reversal in Nelly's role coincides with the portent of a reversal for Heathcliff as well. His vicious — 'sexist' is hardly an adequate word — and vaguely perverse treatment of Isabella forms a grotesque parody of his obsessive pursuit of Cathy, and indicates how easily the fascinating, infantile, 'phallo-eccentric' desire he represents can transform itself into the oppressive phallocentric patriarchy that is its obverse, respect for the law and all: 'I've sometimes relented, from pure lack of invention, in my experiments on what she could endure, and still creep shamefully cringing back! But tell [Linton], also, to set his fraternal and magisterial heart at ease, that I keep strictly within the limits of the law' (p. 184). The emergence of an acute social problematic — defined in terms of law, inheritance and the integrity of the family as an *estate* — is driving the narrative towards a juncture where Heathcliff and Nelly's paths cross, and it is precisely the text's rejection of Heathcliff's *social* project that will disqualify him as a final guardian of the renovated Earnshaw family, and put him on a path towards textual marginalization.

Another index of Isabella as a parodic Cathy, and a further mark of Nelly and Heathcliff's convergence of interest, can be seen in the way Heathcliff and Nelly talk about Isabella in her presence, as if she were not there. Heathcliff insultingly calls her a 'mere slut' (p. 183), repeating Nelly's perception of her entering the Heights as a 'thorough little slattern'.[2] Their discussion of Isabella is reminiscent of Edgar and Nelly's exchanges about, and

in front of, Cathy, and is in fact a prelude to Heathcliff
and Nelly's negotiations concerning Cathy. Neither Heathcliff nor Nelly (nor the text) seems very solicitous of the
feelings of the young women in their charge: when Heathcliff inquires about Cathy's illness, Nelly again 'blamed
her, as she deserved, for bringing it all on herself' (p. 180);
and Nelly is surely right about the 'cruelty and selfishness'
of Heathcliff re-entering Cathy's life, in view of her deteriorating health. Isabella pays only a more immediate and
acute price than Cathy for her attraction to Heathcliff.
This text, it seems, will have its Oedipal seduction played
out in some form, at whatever cost to the women who are
its ambivalent participants.

Yet Isabella parodies Heathcliff and Cathy's relation in
an even more direct way. When Heathcliff, locked out of
the Heights on returning from his death-watch, demands
that Isabella let him in, she enunciates a startlingly effective
mockery of the whole *amour fou* project, a mockery that
momentarily shatters indispensable supports of the textual
ideology, threatening to undermine the 'lived relation' in
which the reader must be held:

> [T] hat's a poor love of yours, that cannot bear a
> shower of snow! We were left at peace in our beds,
> as long as the summer moon shone, but the moment a
> blast of winter returns, you must run for shelter!
> Heathcliff, if I were you, I'd go stretch myself over
> her grave, and die like a faithful dog . . . The world is
> surely not worth living in now, is it? You had distinctly
> impressed on me the idea that Catherine was the whole
> joy of your life — I can't imagine how you think of
> surviving her loss. (p. 217)

This outburst is indeed a discursive cold shower in the
text, and if followed through in any of the subject-positions
constellated in and around the novel (characters, narrators,
'author', 'reader') would revolutionize the reader's relation
to the text. But this speech passes barely noticed beside
the immediately following images of graphic violence

between Heathcliff and Hindley — the knife 'slitting up the flesh' (p. 218) — images that resume the text's obsessive phallicism. In fact, as if to ensure confirmation of the mad desire, the text later informs us that Heathcliff actually was out digging at Catherine's grave in the snow.

With such dearly learned discursive irony, then, it is Isabella who becomes (not Nelly who is) a voice of sanity in the text. This is perhaps because only Isabella, acknowledging her own fascinations, takes up a disinterested, occasionally ironic, relation to phallic power:

> [Hindley] pull(ed) from his waistcoat a curiously constructed pistol, having a double-edged spring knife attached to the barrel ... I surveyed the weapon inquisitively; a hideous notion struck me. How powerful I should be possessing such an instrument! I took it from his hand, and touched the blade. He looked astonished at the expression my face assumed during a brief second. It was not horror, it was covetousness. He snatched the pistol back, jealously; shut the knife, and returned it to its concealment. (p. 171)

Thus, and through no moralism, does Isabella see that 'treachery and violence are spears pointed at both ends' (p. 214). Unlike Nelly, who maintains a surreptitious, 'disarming' control over the text's phallic weaponry when she 'take[s] the shot out of the master's [Hindley's] fowling-piece', Isabella lets the weapon go — back to its 'jealous' owner. Unlike Cathy, who destroys herself through indecision in that irresolvable tension between desire and Law, Isabella, after succumbing to the novel's most misguided infatuation, finally does see and take the only sane course: to exit from the scene of such intense, double-edged phallic obsession. The flight of a pregnant woman from her husband and home, to live and give birth by herself is surely quite a radical moment in this or any other Victorian novel — a moment related with supreme nonchalance by the text, and largely unnoticed in the outraged critical fulminations against the demonic Heathcliff or the irresponsible Cathy. It is Isabella's decision here that most profoundly opens this text to 'other' alternatives and completely different subject-positions. But these alternatives are entirely indigestible within the narrative, so that Isabella's departure from the Heights via the Grange, from Heathcliff via Nelly, is also an irreversible exit from the text. It is not the strong, phallic-autonomous woman who will find a new place in this text, but the weak little boy, her wounded son.

When Heathcliff does visit Cathy for their final encounter, there is no explicit description of sexual activity, but the language of the text is charged with a sense of 'inhuman' transgression:

'Do come to me, Heathcliff.'
In her eagerness she rose, and supported herself on the arm of the chair. At that earnest appeal, he turned to her, looking absolutely desperate. His eyes wide, and wet at last, flashed fiercely on her; his breast heaved convulsively. An instant they held asunder; and then how they met I hardly saw, but Catherine made a spring, and he caught her, and they were locked in an embrace from which I thought my mistress would never be released alive. In fact, to my eyes, she seemed directly insensible. He flung himself into the nearest seat, and on my approaching hurriedly to ascertain if she had fainted, he gnashed at me, and foamed like a mad dog, and gathered her to him with greedy jealousy. I did not feel as if I were in the company of a creature of my own species; it appeared that he would not understand, although I spoke to him; so, I stood off, and held my tongue, in great perplexity. (p. 197)

Whatever the 'empirical' status of this event, the discursive electricity here produces the *effect* of a sexual connection. In the text's symbolic order, this connection, the proximate cause of Catherine's death, is certainly more important and disruptive than any previous contact — a virtual consummation of the Oedipal seduction. Even Nelly's indefatigable textual voice is shocked into silence. That this consummation occurs under Nelly's management, at a point where it is 'really' restricted and futile, indicates Nelly's capacity to absorb and deflect the most subversive libidinal drives, and her flexibility as an agent who adapts to narrative pressures, shifting from opposition to, to co-optation of, the antagonistic project that Heathcliff so insistently enacts within the text.

This carefully crafted coincidence of contradictory tendencies figures the processes of the text's consumption and production. Critics have remarked that the reader of *Wuthering Heights* tends to feel constant sympathy for Heathcliff, even if often *despite* his destructive actions.[3] Indeed, precisely at such moments, the sympathy appears as a 'problem'. Nelly, on the other hand, effectively solicits an unnoticed 'natural' sympathy through her 'common-sense' discourse and narrative control. The simultaneous identification with the disruptive wish-fulfilment figure (Heathcliff) and the pacifying voice of the textual censor (Nelly) helps to ease the reader's consumption of the textual fantasy. This structure may itself echo a process of textual production through which a feminine authorial ego obtains a sublimated fantasy satisfaction for an Oedipal desire cathected on a displaced father-figure. The structure of the encounter scene, then, is the structure of the management of desire, and figures the textual situation, even as it pre-figures the text's ending — shifting the textual problematic to a new stage that sets final determinations for the resolution of the narrative dynamic.

6 The Abolition of Characters in 'the Name-of-the-Father, but . . .'

I should say, not that the heroes have disappeared
because Brecht has banished them from his plays, but
that even as the heroes they are, and in the play
itself, the play makes them impossible, abolishes
them, their consciousness and its false dialectic. This
reduction is not the effect of the action alone . . .
it is not even merely the result of the play appreciated
as an unresolved story; it is not at the level of detail
or of continuity, but at the deeper level of the play's
structural dynamic.

Louis Althusser, *For Marx* (1970, p. 148)

If the text has forced Nelly out of the position of phallic
mother, upholder of the incest taboo, into a conjunctural
connivance with Heathcliff's phallo-eccentric desire, we
might expect the narrative to motivate Heathcliff towards
an analogous reversal. And indeed after Cathy's death,
Heathcliff, who was able to achieve a kind of final, con-
summative contact with the Earnshaw daughter only with
Nelly's reluctant assistance, himself becomes the unlikely
proponent of an attempt to 'Linton-ize' the Earnshaws in
the sexual sense, as a step towards his goal of final social
revenge. As the narrative begins to look towards the future,
as carried in the fate of the heirs (Cathy Linton, Linton
Heathcliff and Hareton Earnshaw), Nelly makes one direct

attempt to retrieve the 'last of the ancient Earnshaw stock', whom she emphatically calls '*my* Hareton' (p. 134), from Heathcliff's influence. On the occasion of Hindley's death, 'resolved to . . . assist in the last duties of the dead', she asks Edgar Linton's permission to go to the Heights:

> Mr. Linton was extremely reluctant to consent, but I pleaded eloquently for the friendless condition in which [Hindley] lay; and I said my old master and foster brother had a claim on my services as strong as his own. Besides, I reminded him that the child, Hareton, was his wife's nephew, and, in the absence of nearer kin, he ought to act as its guardian; and he ought to and must inquire how the property was left, and look over the concerns of his brother-in-law.
>
> He was unfit for attending to such matters then, but he bade me speak to his lawyer; and at length permitted me to go. (p. 229)

In Nelly's characteristically self-effacing discourse, a 'besides' introduces the most important concern — the heir and the inheritance. At the Heights, she tells Heathcliff that Linton 'has ordered me to take [Hareton]' (p. 231) — a quite active construal of Linton's 'extreme reluctance' to let her even go to the Heights, his half-hearted 'bid' that she speak to the lawyer, and the lawyer's own discouragements (p. 229). But Heathcliff is able to keep control of Hareton, by threatening to recall his own son, Linton Heathcliff, whom Edgar, if not Nelly, is more interested in keeping away from Heathcliff; Heathcliff can also prove his rights as the mortgagee and new 'master' of Wuthering Heights. Through his contact with Cathy as well as his shrewd accumulation of capital, Heathcliff has established a decisive power over the Earnshaw family and can make a counter-claim on Hareton as emphatic as Nelly's: 'Now, my bonny lad, you are *mine*!' (p. 230).

Heathcliff wants to take revenge on Hindley through Hareton, forcing the latter, whom he has already reduced to cultural poverty by forbidding the curate's reading and writing lessons (p. 134), to 'live in his own house as a servant deprived of the advantage of wages' (p. 231). But this project can only be ironically successful, precisely because it creates a Hareton in Heathcliff's own image: 'And we'll see if one tree won't grow as crooked as another, with the same wind to twist it!' (p. 230). It is not Heathcliff 'himself', but the libidinal power he figures, that has achieved an irrevocable stake in the Earnshaw family, and in so far as during the thirteen years of Heathcliff's 'mastery' after Hindley's death Hareton becomes the new image of that power, neither Heathcliff nor Nelly will be allowed to stand in his way.

We get a hint of the novel's inevitable outcome when Cathy Linton decides that she's old enough — that is, enough of a 'woman' (p. 234) — to go to Penistone Crags, and ends up being led by Hareton, who 'opened the mysteries of the Fairy cave' to her (p. 243). Resting at the Heights, she finds him ('I'll see thee damned, before I be *thy* servant!' (p. 239)) and the servants (Softly, Miss . . . I was never hired to serve you' (p. 239)) too uppity for her tastes, and can hardly believe that '*He*', so awkward and brutish, is her cousin; but 'she seemed perfectly at home' (p. 237) for a moment none the less. It is to her 'rude-bred' but 'well-made, athletic . . . good looking' guide on her maiden exploration of the caves and the crags that she will return (p. 240).

By the time Isabella dies, and her son Linton returns to the narrative, the wheel of Heathcliff's social fortune has fully turned. He has now himself attained the income and status of a local 'gentleman', the proprietor of what Nelly calls 'the next best[house] in the neighbourhood' (p. 252). He has also earned a reputation as 'a cruel hard landlord to his tenants', and, with the help of efficient 'female management', as a more respectable householder than his predecessor: 'the house, inside, had regained its ancient aspect of comfort under female management; and the scenes of riot common in Hindley's time were not now enacted within its walls' (p. 242). But his move from

oppressed farm worker to avenging tyrant cannot be
complete until he gets control of the best house in the
neighbourhood as well, and to ensure his legal claim to
the Linton property, he must embrace the character most
unlike himself — his son Linton — and turn him into
Hareton Earnshaw's master:

> [H]e's *mine*, and I want the triumph of seeing *my*
> descendants fairly lord of their estates; my child
> hiring their children, to till their father's lands for
> wages — That is the sole consideration which can
> make me endure the whelp ... I've ordered Hareton
> to obey him: and in fact, I've arranged every thing
> with a view to preserve the superior and the gentle-
> man in him, above his associates. (p. 255)

Having encouraged the boy Heathcliff himself calls a
'whey-faced whining wretch' (p. 256) to lord it over 'the
last of the ancient Earnshaw stock', Heathcliff must then
try to enforce an equally uncharacteristic project — a
marriage between this 'puling chicken' (p. 254) and the
young Cathy Linton, who reinstantiates the energy and
independence of her namesake. As Heathcliff explains it
to Nelly:

> 'My design is ... [t]hat the two cousins may fall
> in love, and get married. I'm acting generously to
> your master; his young chit has no expectations and
> should she second my wishes, she'll be provided for,
> at once, as joint successor with Linton [Heathcliff].'
> 'If Linton died', I answered, 'and his life is quite
> uncertain, Catherine would be the heir.'
> 'No, she would not', he said. 'There is no clause in
> the will to secure it so; his property would go on to
> me; but to prevent disputes, I desire their union, and
> am resolved to bring it about.' (pp. 262–3)

Heathcliff's plan even has considerable appeal to Edgar
Linton, who, if he does not want his daughter seeing
Heathcliff or visiting the Heights, does not mind the idea

of her striking up a romance with the 'weakling' nephew
(p. 247) whose 'pale, delicate, effeminate' form (p. 245) is
an exaggerated textual echo of Edgar's own. So Edgar
agrees to weekly meetings between Cathy and her cousin,
on neutral ground and under Nelly's 'guardianship':

> [F]or June found [Edgar] still declining; and, though
> he had set aside, yearly, a portion of his income for
> my young lady's fortune, he had a natural desire that
> she might retain — or, at least, return in a short time
> to — the house of her ancestors; and he considered
> her only prospect of doing that was by a union with
> his heir; he had no idea that the latter was failing
> almost as fast as himself; nor had any one, I believe.
> (pp. 315 6)

No one, that is, except Nelly, who tries to persuade Cathy
that young Linton's health is deteriorating:

> 'You think *he is* better in health, then?' I said.
> 'Yes,' she answered; ' . . . He is not tolerably well, as
> he told me to tell papa, but he's better . . .'
> 'There you differ with me, Miss Cathy', I remarked;
> 'I should conjecture him to be far worse.' (p. 320)

Because Nelly recognizes young Linton's precarious physical
condition, and sees the possibility of Cathy Linton (under
her 'guardianship') holding the Grange, she has no interest
in uniting the families at the Heights and tries to derail
the Cathy-Linton romance.

At this point, then, Heathcliff aligns himself with a
blatant libidinal mismatch for the worst kind of patriarchal
elitist purposes, while Nelly works against this project of
the two fathers, attempting with consistent discipline to
discourage Cathy's responses to her cousin. It is Edgar who
is persuaded, by Cathy's pleas and young Linton's corre-
spondence, to allow them to continue to meet. Heathcliff
has allied himself with Edgar in trying to promote —
against Nelly, who tries to prevent — a perverse repetition
of the Catherine Earnshaw-Edgar Linton marriage. Heath-

cliff himself recognizes the incongruence of pushing Linton on Cathy, as well as the suitability of Hareton, his own analogue, as an alternative.

> I am afraid, Nelly, I shall lose my labour ... Miss Catherine, as the ninny [Linton] calls her, will discover his value, and send him to the devil. Now, if it had been Hareton — do you know that twenty times a day I covet Hareton, with all his degradation? ... But I think he's safe from *her* love. (p. 265)

> I've a pleasure in him! ... He has satisfied my expectations ... and I can sympathize with his feelings, having felt them myself — I know what he suffers now, for instance, exactly. (p. 267)

All these considerations have a direct bearing on the complex inheritance situation, which, not surprisingly, only Nelly and Heathcliff seem to understand. There is some ambiguity (and critical disagreement) about whether Heathcliff needs to make Cathy Linton marry his own son in order to take control of the Grange. Old Linton's will had stipulated the following order of inheritance: Edgar, then his sons, then Isabella, then her sons. Edgar's *daughter* is passed over, first, in favour of Isabella, and then in favour of Isabella and Heathcliff's son Linton. Thus, Heathcliff will take effective control of the Grange estate, for some time at least, whether or not his son marries Cathy, *as long as* Edgar Linton dies before Linton Heathcliff. Edgar Linton admits this above, and on his deathbed, when he 'divine[s] that one of his enemy's purposes was to secure the personal property [the money saved for Cathy out of the rents], *as well as* the estate, to his son, or rather himself' (p. 342, my emphasis). But as Nelly again points out, Edgar is 'ignorant how nearly he and his nephew would quit the world together' (p. 342).

It is Linton Heathcliff's failing health that makes the marriage with Cathy such an urgent matter for Heathcliff, who knows that his dream of leaving his son master of the estates is futile ('that lad . . . seems determined to beat me' (p. 326)), and that young Linton might well die before Edgar ('and I'd thank his uncle to be quick, and go before him' (p. 326)). Heathcliff's confident claim of his own rights should his son die, in response to Nelly's shrewd challenge above, is somewhat disingenuous, for if young Linton's legal claim to the Grange supersedes Cathy's, it is not so clear that Heathcliff's does.[1] This is precisely the 'dispute' that Heathcliff seeks to prevent, and it is by using the *marriage laws* to get control of Cathy's personal property that he seeks to prevent it. Heathcliff prevents Edgar from leaving Cathy's personal funds in trusteeship, by bribing the lawyer to arrive late at Edgar's deathbed. It hardly matters what the inheritance laws say, since Cathy's marriage transfers all the personal wealth she has just inherited to her new husband, who immediately leaves it to Heathcliff. Cathy is thus left dispossessed and completely dependent on Heathcliff, with no autonomous means to pursue, against the combined forces of the new 'master' of this territory and the local lawyer who has 'sold himself' thereto (p. 344), any legal redress she might merit. The law here, as Nelly recognizes, is power: 'at any rate, Catherine, destitute of cash and friends, cannot disturb his possession' (p. 356).

Thus, Heathcliff has reversed his position to co-operate with Edgar in a libidinal project, because of his commitment to a carefully conceived social project, just as Nelly had previously 'turned' to co-operate with Heathcliff's desire, for her own kind of 'socio-political' reasons. *Wuthering Heights*, in fact, is a highly charged 'Gothic-Romantic' text whose major transformations are determined as much by its social as by its libidinal instance, by its 'infrastructure' as much as by its 'unconscious'. Heathcliff and Nelly are not just surrogates for phallo-eccentric father and surrogate mother in an Oedipal drama, they are the 'holes in the social cell', through which the family's relation to society and a class structure will be rearticulated.

But the project of the *text* is not that of any of its

characters. Heathcliff may seek revenge on Hindley through Hareton, but Heathcliff is himself in the text by the grace of a previous (step)father, on behalf of a primal Father, whose name is also Hareton, and whose interests he *will* be made to serve. Heathcliff may 'forget' his relationship to the Earnshaws, but the text does not. His libidinal task is the displaced Oedipal seduction of the Earnshaw daughter, which he enacts in a metaphorically strong but 'really' (in terms of the novel's diegetic 'reality') weak form with Catherine, and which he ironically makes possible in a more sublimated but more durable form by bringing Cathy into the house where Hareton will be sure to outlive young Linton; Heathcliff's specific social task is the *unification* of the two families. Once these two tasks are accomplished, Heathcliff's larger project of revenge is suddenly drained of its interest/cathexis and virtually disappears: 'It's a poor conclusion, is it not . . . An absurd termination to my violent exertions? I get levers and mattocks to demolish the two houses, and train myself to be capable of working like Hercules, and when everything is ready, and in my power, I find the will to lift a slate off either roof has vanished' (p. 392).

Edgar may want the Cathy-Linton marriage as the most secure foundation of Cathy's economic future; Cathy herself might see Linton as a logical mate, preferable to the illiterate and class-inferior Hareton, and — as she indicates even while Heathcliff is kidnapping her into the marriage — compatible with the love of her father, with her father's desire and her father's law: '*I am* afraid now . . . because if I stay, papa will be miserable; and how can I endure making him miserable . . . Mr. Heathcliff, *let* me go home! I promise to marry Linton — papa would like me to, and I love him — and why should you force me to do what I'll willingly do of myself?' (p. 332). But the text is interested in, and works in the interests of, another father, and another father's desire(s). Cathy is not brought to the Heights in order to restore the possession of the Grange to the Linton daughter, or the half-Linton son,

but to bring it to the 'last of the ancient Earnshaw stock'.[2]
Cathy's 'heaven' is no more congruent with Linton Heathcliff's than was Catherine Earnshaw's with Edgar's: 'He
[Linton Heathcliff] wanted to lie in an ecstasy of peace;
I wanted all to sparkle, and dance in a glorious jubilee. I
said his heaven would be only half-alive, and he said mine
would be drunk; I said I should fall asleep in his, and he
said he could not breathe in mine' (p. 302).

In *Wuthering Heights*, the sadism of the weak tends to
be particularly despicable, and if *in* the text Cathy is quite
viciously abused by Linton Heathcliff's mean, vaguely
sexual sadism, he is perhaps the figure most ridiculed and
abused *by* the text. Once his marriage to Cathy assures the
unification of the families, the text quickly — and with no
particular regret — disposes of him. Cathy's attention is
then turned to her more proletarian cousin — not in spite,
but because of this class difference. The marriage of the
grandson and granddaughter of 'the old master' will make
something new of the Earnshaw family.

Beginning with Heathcliff, then, the text begins to
'abolish' its own heroes, to cancel the 'false dialectic'
of their characterological consciousness. Heathcliff 'becomes' the Earnshaw father only too completely; he
turns from a figure of phallic energy into a figure of
impotent rage, who is chastised and quelled by young
Cathy much as old Earnshaw was by his Catherine:

> His [Earnshaw's] peevish reproofs wakened in her
> [Catherine] a naughty delight to provoke him; she
> was never so happy as when [she was] ... doing just
> what her father hated most, showing how her preten-
> ded insolence ... had more power over Heathcliff
> than his kindness: how the boy would do *her* bidding
> in anything, and *his* only when it suited his own
> inclination. (p. 52)

> 'Hareton and I are friends now; and I shall tell him
> about you!'
> The master [Heathcliff] seemed confounded a

moment: he grew pale, and rose up, eyeing her all the while, with an expression of mortal hate.

'If you strike me, Hareton will strike you!' she said, 'so you may as well sit down.'

'If Hareton does not turn you out of the room, I'll strike him to Hell', thundered Heathcliff . . .

Hareton tried under his breath to persuade her to go.

'Drag her away!' he cried savagely. 'Are you staying to talk?' . . .

'He'll not obey you, wicked man, any more!' said Catherine. (p. 389)

The difference between these two tauntings is of course important: in the second passage, Cathy Linton is not playing on paternal jealousy, but denouncing the theft of her and Hareton's 'land and money' (pp. 388–9). And there seems a more unexpected sympathy between Hareton and Heathcliff — 'ties stronger than reason could break' (p. 391) — which impel Hareton to insist that Cathy forgo any further attack. But there is also the common image of the daughter positioning herself between father and son, and taking control of both, at once teasing and pacifying phallic power. Cathy Linton, who turns towards the relation with Hareton, will be more successful at this than Catherine Earnshaw, who turned away from the relation with Heathcliff. In the event, phallic energy grown stale, unmodulated by the feminine, loses any aspect of a liberating anarchy and becomes a purely repressive force — as caricatured in the absurd patriarchalism of Joseph, whose trees Heathcliff is defending against young Cathy in the above argument.

When Heathcliff approaches this point of masculine staleness, the text banishes him from interfering in the world of Hareton and Cathy, a world he helped to create and will not now be allowed to despoil. Indeed, Heathcliff banishes himself to a kind of preternatural realm, in a gradual process of reconnection with his own youthful sexuality, which haunts him in the form of Cathy's ghost.

At the cost of a cut hand, Heathcliff finally makes it through the window of his bedchamber, this text's wet, and sometimes bloody, passage:

> I could not think him dead — but his face and throat were washed with rain; the bed-clothes dripped, and he was perfectly still. The lattice, flapping to and fro, had grazed one hand that rested on the sill — no blood trickled from the broken skin, and when I put my fingers to it, I could doubt no more — he was dead and stark! (pp. 410—11)

Nelly's intentions, too, are cancelled by the text. She cannot prevent the union of Hareton and Cathy, any more than she could the short-lived marriage of Cathy and Linton. She had no interest in the latter because it was not hers, but Heathcliff's, task to unite the two families under the Earnshaw name; she would just as soon have lived peacefully within an autonomous and ascendant Linton estate. But, if she tries to prevent the Cathy-Linton marriage, it is not because she exactly favours a Cathy-Hareton union. Hareton is a little too 'rude-bred', and their marriage would be slightly too libidinally charged, too reminiscent of the sexual energy of the Heathcliff-Catherine affair that so discomfited Nelly. In fact the Hareton-Cathy marriage is the successful reprise of the frustrated Heathcliff-Catherine affair, and the vindication of Catherine Earnshaw's desire. Catherine is present in both of the new lovers, but especially in Hareton, the Earnshaw descendant who thus becomes the text's final 'androgynous' figure — a phallic presence strongly modulated by feminine desire: '[P]erhaps you have remarked that their eyes are precisely similar, and they are those of Catherine Earnshaw. The present Catherine has no other likeness to her, except a breadth of forehead, and a certain arch of the nostril ... With Hareton the resemblance is carried farther: it is singular, at all times' (p. 392).

Besides, between Edgar's death and Heathcliff's, Nelly is unsure whether she will ever regain the kind of pseudo-maternal management role (which seems such an important stake for her) in *any* of the inheritors' lives. Heathcliff, Cathy's 'new father' (p. 352), has refused to let Cathy stay at the Grange, and has banished Nelly from the Heights, telling her: 'I want none of your prying at my house!' (p. 110). So, in a manoeuvre to win the new daughter away from the influence of the new father and son at the Heights, Nelly turns to the eligible — and for her purposes eminently appropriate — bachelor at hand, telling Lockwood: 'I can see no remedy, at present, unless [Cathy] could marry again; and that scheme, it does not come within my province to arrange' (p. 361). Less than fifty words later in the text, Nelly proves to be no slouch at arranging such things, as Lockwood tells us: 'I went to the Heights as I proposed; my housekeeper entreated me to bear a little note from her to her young lady, and I did not refuse, for the worthy woman was not conscious of anything odd in her request' (p. 362).

It is Lockwood, of course, the reader's analogue, who is somewhat unconscious of Nelly's manipulations. And the text emphasizes here, in one last and crucial instance, that he is not an 'extraneous' narrator, but — like all the other narrators in this text — a participant in the narrative, caught up in a continuing struggle for influence over the Earnshaw family's fate through its heirs. Nelly's address to Lockwood has always been not just explicitly descriptive, but also implicitly imperative; hers is not just a narrative of events, but also an attempt to involve Lockwood *in* events that are still unfolding, culminating in this 'odd request'.[3] Lockwood has already been qualified by the text for the task Nelly is here proposing: this is, after all, the same Lockwood who plugged the hole in the window against the appeal of Catherine Earnshaw's spirit, thereby enacting the counterphobic mechanism of patriarchal law, and protecting his narcissistic enclosure within the space of the phallic mother. So, afraid lest a romance between Hareton and Cathy, with Heathcliff as master, might shut her out permanently, Nelly tries to intervene with Lockwood, who seems the perfect candidate for her match-making: effete, bookish and absolutely gullible. He would moderate Cathy's desire to 'sparkle and dance in a glorious jubilee', would — more effectively than Hareton — open the way to greater social respectability, and would probably take the 'worthy woman' herself along as lady-in-waiting. One can almost hear, in Lockwood's rather self-aggrandizing tones, the woman who would 'frame high notions of my birth' sharing his disappointment:

> Living among clowns and misanthropists, she [Cathy] probably cannot appreciate a better class of people, when she meets them.
> . . . What a realization of something more romantic than a fairy tale it would have been for Mrs. Linton Heathcliff, had she and I struck up an attachment, as her good nurse desired, and migrated together into the stirring atmosphere of the town! (p. 368)

There is a symptomatic 'slip' in the voice of the text here. Lockwood now seems to take for granted Nelly's matchmaking intentions ('as her good nurse desired'), which he had discounted a few pages earlier ('the worthy woman was not conscious of anything odd in her request'). This slight inconsistency in the relation between the textual voice and the voice of the primary narrator, indicates, and calls the critical reader's attention to, a discrepancy that is always there, and that is in fact constitutive of the text's narrational frame.

With these remarks, Lockwood suddenly rejects his earlier touted 'misanthropy' for the sociable atmosphere of the town, which he imagines as offering a temptation to Cathy Linton much like that which Edgar's 'petted' life at Thrushcross Grange offered to Catherine Earnshaw. And Nelly, whose design Lockwood now recognizes, tries to interfere with Cathy and Hareton as she did with Catherine and Heathcliff. But the new Cathy is not drawn to Lockwood or to whatever his high society might offer, and is completely oblivious to his imaginary seduction by letter.

Cathy's knee, where Lockwood 'adroitly' (p. 363) drops the note, does not respond to the message from Nelly's pen as a romantic overture. At this point, Cathy is wrapped up in an irreversible relationship with Hareton, a charged love—hate battle in which her books are tokens of an inequality of social power that frustrates a libidinal connection. Only the restoration of a socio-cultural equality, achieved across the pages of books, will enable the marriage that finally restores a general, if precarious, equilibrium to this family and text. The little sub-drama with Lockwood confirms the text's project by 'cancelling' Nelly's intentions as it did Heathcliff's. Cathy — that is, the Earnshaw family — can no more have a future with Lockwood than she could with young Linton.

The text 'abolishes' its heroes and their 'false consciousness', then, but this abolition is not quite symmetrical. If Heathcliff passes out of the Earnshaw family, Nelly Dean retrenches herself within, making the most of the Hareton-Cathy match — a match with which she must live, and with which she can live after Heathcliff dies. With 'the lawful master and the ancient stock . . . restored to their rights' (p. 411), Nelly, 'patriarchy's paradigmatic housekeeper', is the appropriate agent to oversee the necessary social and cultural consolidation of the new Earnshaw family. Nelly superintends Cathy's reading and writing lessons with Hareton, and acts as the trustee of their estate — the combined Earnshaw and Linton properties. She moves them down to the Grange, away from the spectral terrain of the Heights, which is haunted in one way or another by the spirits of Heathcliff and Cathy, or 'such ghosts as choose to inhabit it' (p. 413). At the Grange, Hareton can learn his letters, and the newlyweds' energies can be channelled into respectable forms under Nelly's management. Separated, for a time at least, from the unsettling influence of the Heights, a calm domesticity replaces obsessive desire, and the cycle of family life can begin again, in the absence of the father and the father's disruptive demand.

The father's phallic desire has already had its play in this text, and will not exactly go away, but in its strongest form — as Cathy and Heathcliff's love — will be placed 'out of this world'. The repressed has returned, again to be banished, but now not so far away. The primal lovers — up at the Heights wandering, and down in their graves in 'unquiet slumbers' — literally envelop their sublimated analogues at the Grange. The primal family — the daughter in between the father's desire and law — sleeps uneasily beneath its secondary, stable revision — Cathy, Hareton and Nelly. Desire has at once been exiled in its taboo form with Heathcliff and Cathy, in order to permit social stability, and at the same time has been socialized *within* the Hareton-Cathy relationship, where desire does not conflict with, but passes through, law, property, marriage, the phallic mother, the pen and the book. Heathcliff and Catherine, leaving the latter's diary to scamper under the dairy woman's cloak, have become Hareton and Cathy studying their letters under the watchful veiled phallic I/eye of Nelly Dean, who puts the 'i' back in its proper place:

> [T]hey were . . . as busy as possible, in their several occupations of pupil and teacher. I came in to sit with them, after I had done my work . . . You know, they both appeared, in a measure, my children: I had been proud of one, and now, I was sure, the other would be a source of equal satisfaction . . . His brightening mind brightened his features, and added spirit and nobility to their aspect — I could hardly fancy it the same individual I had beheld on the day I discovered my little lady at Wuthering Heights, after her expedition to the Crags. (p. 391)

Much of the final, epiphanic quality of *Wuthering Heights* derives from this sense of the triumphal escape of desire from the world, and its concurrent, residual endurance as a constituent force in the world. But if desire is to endure, it must be managed in a socially survivable form. Thus, the

Earnshaw family, and the father's desire, is finally reconstituted, and returns to the world in a new formulation
that we might call 'the Name-of-the-Father, but . . . ': the
Earnshaw family, but under the Linton roof; Hareton
Earnshaw, but not he of the primal year 1500, not he of
the 'crumbling griffins and shameless little boys', not
even he of the 'expedition to the Crags'; Hareton Earnshaw,
but Catherine Linton, too; Hareton Earnshaw, but under
the tutelage of Nelly Dean.

7   The Hol(e)y Family: Exiling Desire and Housekeeping Ideology

The final structure of *Wuthering Heights*, then, separates primary from sublimated desire, exiling the former, and socializing the latter within a family now no longer disrupted by the father's seduction, but stabilized under the phallic mother's 'guardianship'. Desire and Law both 'win', producing a state, not of compromise, but of modified antagonism, in which each surrenders some ground to the other: the father's Desire — figured in Heathcliff and Cathy's ghosts — remains as a continuing, parallel, other-dimensional presence, shadowing and rendering precarious the reconstituted regime of the father's Law — of which Nelly is the 'trustee'. But, as the novel consistently acknowledges, the father's Law is embedded in a system of 'real' property, political legislation and social relations. At stake in this newly resolved antagonism was never just the family's mode of adjusting to the tumultuous return of a repressed Oedipal desire; the family also has to adjust to the invasive appearance of a powerful, disruptive force that threatens the coherence of those social relations on which the family depends, and which it must therefore help to reproduce. In casting the Oedipal drama with surrogates who are household workers, *Wuthering Heights* rudely tears open the 'holes in the [family as] social cell', and allows us to consider how the narrative's resolution figures a tenuous repair of these sweaty, if not bloody, passages.

From the standpoint of an early nineteenth-century rural, parsonist ideology, *Wuthering Heights* might be seen as offering the dream of a social family in which the destabilizing, 'demonically' masculine, capitalist energies are either/both exiled or/and assigned a dominated position within rural petty-aristocratic structures. But *Wuthering Heights* also offers an extraordinary, anticipatory image of the fraught relationship between, and preferred but precarious separation of, two social spheres — the sphere of social production, in which economically valuable goods and services are produced, and the sphere of social reproduction, in which the relations of production are reproduced through the ideological formation of social subjects — as well as of the family's crucial role within the latter. For the family in *Wuthering Heights* is certainly a significant institution ideologically as well as economically — indeed, it is a site of both economic and ideological *production*. The family in this text is what Althusserian theory would call an 'ideological apparatus'[1] — that is, a social mechanism for producing appropriate class subjects, who are prepared to assume their place in the system of social relations that supports a given mode of production:

> [T]he totality of social relations that comprise a society are founded upon one central cluster of relations [−] ... the relations of production. The family is ultimately dependent upon the dominant mode of production for its existence and form ...
>
> The family has a special role to play in the ideological reproduction of the relations of production. The state (through its educational and media apparatus) is a complement but not a substitute for the family in this regard. For it is the family, and above all the mother that produces willing participants for the social order. The early socialization of children is primarily the mother's task. Eventually young adults must be produced who have internalized a repertoire of attitudes and perceptual structures that enable

them to self-actualize willingly in an adjusted manner
within bourgeois relations . . .

The labour of the family unit reproduces simultaneously components of labour power and the
relations of production. It follows from this that the
function of the family unit within the capitalist mode
of production is a reproductive one, but that this
function has both an economic and an ideological
aspect.[2]

In part, the structural transformations of the family in
Wuthering Heights are symptomatic of a crisis in the
internal relationship of economic and ideological functions
within the social family, a crisis provoked by the pressures
of an insurgent mode of production which increasingly
locates economic power outside the family. The final
familial structure of *Wuthering Heights* is, in modern
economic terms, the result of a merger and retrenchment
in response to a particularly dramatic 'leveraged buyout'.
Of course, the families in this novel are not modern cor-
porations, and the 'retrenchment' in question involves
precisely a redefinition of function that emphasizes the
family's survival in terms of its ideological, rather than its
economic, tasks. Still, Heathcliff intrudes on the novel's
original family regime not just as an agent of the father's
desire, but also as an agent of a disruptive capitalist dynamic
that corrodes and transforms traditional family structures.
As E.P. Thompson points out, the appearance on the
English social scene between 1780 and 1830 of masses of
'free' labouring children — including homeless 'waifs'
like the young Heathcliff — was the result of transformations in the mode of production that forced children
from impoverished homes to survive outside their families,
transformations like 'the fact of specialization itself, the
increasing differentiation of economic roles, and the
break-up of the family economy'.[3]

Indeed, Emily Brontë's father was himself one of those
children. We have mentioned his reactionary posturing as

a cleric in England, but Patrick Brontë was born into an Irish peasant family, and began his working life as a blacksmith's helper and a weaver's apprentice. It was during this time that he took to memorizing Milton's poetry — including the whole of *Paradise Lost* — as a kind of poetic compensation for his proletarian plight. But his imaginary sights were set higher, and when he heard himself referred to as 'a gentleman by nature',[4] he set out to make good that judgement. Like an exaggerated real version of Stendhal's fictional Julien Sorel, it was through a literary and clerical education — through, that is, his entrance into the ideological apparatus of the Church — that he began his rise to the status of a militant defender of the faith and the propertied classes. As Charlotte described him, his problem was — again like that of Julien Sorel — that 'he had missed his vocation: he should have been a soldier, and circumstances had made him a priest.'[5] The same circumstances also made him a poet: 'To console himself for a missed military career, Patrick Brontë took to writing poetry — just as he consoled himself for the menial tasks of his boyhood by learning Milton by heart.'[6]

These observations may give us another angle on the sense in which Emily Brontë is, in Gilbert and Gubar's terms, 'Milton's daughter', locked in an agonistic struggle with a literary 'forefather'.[7] The word that passes through this family's (fore)fathers is perhaps 'radically revised' but not exactly 'corrected' or 'reversed' by this daughter, in so far as that word is the law of ideological submission, of imaginary identification with a structure of social order. It is more exact, and very different, to say that she is 'Milton's admirer's daughter',[8] since it is the Brontë father whose particular kind of admiration for Milton is in another sense the radical revision of the poetic forefather's books of rebellion. Again, perhaps, this daughter is caught between the two fathers, or between the contrary pressures of the father's demand. The antithetical figuration of the father's Desire and Law in this text is certainly inextricably bound to the ambivalent figures of ideologically rebellious and submissive working children; and the resolution the text offers them is quite clear: the subordination of rebellion within ideological order.

These observations certainly do render pathetically ironical the Reverend Brontë's attacks on, and obsessive fear of, the rebellious weavers of his Yorkshire parishes, and — more relevant to this analysis — gives quite another significance for the 'pen-' that appears throughout the semiotic geography of this text. For perhaps the most heavily traversed site in *Wuthering Heights*'s own signifying 'Pennine' chain is the word 'Penistone'. This word's sexual-semiotic reverberance, constantly on the tip of the text's tongue (' "Then I can go, too, when I am a woman?" ... "Now, am I old enough to go to Penistone Craggs?" ' was the constant question in her mouth' (p. 234)), goes beyond even the obvious marker of the first five letters: 'stone' itself derives from the Indo-European base '*stāi-*', meaning 'to become thick, compress, stiffen, whence Gr. *stear*, fat, L. *stipare*, to compress, *stilla*, a drop', and has the archaic meaning of 'a testicle'.[9]

But 'Penistone' also carries a clear socio-semiotic inscription. 'Penistone' is the name of a small town in the West Riding, a centre for the production of a coarse, cheap cloth, of the same name.[10] It derives from 'penny', and 'penny-stone', probably meaning 'a penny a stone', with 'stone' signifying the British measure of weight equal to fourteen pounds. 'Penny', to complete the circle, derives from the Latin '*pannus*', meaning 'cloth (used as a medium of exchange)'.[11] The 'Crags' are also part of 'Peniston Quarry', which provided millstone grit for buildings near the Haworth parsonage, and the 'cave under the Crags' is a tunnelled grit face. According to local tradition, anyone going through the tunnel would marry in a year; in fact, 'it was a common belief that all caves and hollows in the earth were inhabited by fairies.'[12]

Thus, this one word is a singularly overdetermined textual conjuncture, traversed by psycho-sexual and socio-economic significances, a site of discursive and economic

work. It rings with the echoes of those hollows, which for
some women — like Nelly and Emily Brontë — remained
empty of their legendary promise, filled only with the
sprites of their own imaginary creating; it rings, too, with
inextricably mingled echoes of the father — not only, or
even primarily, in its phallicism, but in its evocation of the
conflicted class reality of the Haworth district, in terms so
appropriate to the conflicted subject history of a former
weaver's apprentice.

It is easier to see the sexo-semiotics of this word, and
this greater visibility actually obscures its semio-ideological
significance; philologically, it is the first four letters of the
word that form its initial seme, or unit of meaning, even if
the first five letters press more insistently for recognition.
This word, then, offers itself for reading much as does the
text as a whole — its psycho-sexual instance is more
'obvious' than its socio-ideological instance, although, as
we have seen, the crucial narrative transformations are
at least as much determined by the latter as by the
former.

At stake in this text is the changing role of the family
in response to the economic and ideological crises of
class society. The text's resolution gives, not a 'reflection'
of a real, but a 'production' of an imaginary ideal solution
for the family's role in a society increasingly dominated
by the turbulent dynamics of capital. The antithetical
demand of the Father's Desire and Law are echoed in the
antithetical demand of capital, which seeks both continually to transform the social universe at will — through
mobilizing the 'free' labour-power of workers forced off
the land — and to maintain a constant orderly reproduction of the social relations of class domination and
submission — requiring the appropriate ideological pacification of those same restless workers. The 'perfect'
solution to this problem — nowhere exactly realized, if
everywhere imagined — is the separation, tendentially
coincidental with a gender division, of the social sphere of
the production of value from the social sphere of the

reproduction of the relations of production, with the latter given an imaginary stability and protection from the vicissitudes of the former:

> In feudal societies, the family was co-terminous with the basic unit of production, and as such domestic labour was embedded within the labour of general production. Capitalism entailed fundamental changes in the mode of production and these structural changes have altered the position of the domestic labourer within production . . .
>
> With the advent of industrial capitalism, the general labour process was split into two discrete units; a domestic and an industrial unit. The character of the work performed in each was fundamentally different. The domestic unit reproduced labour power for the labour market. The industrial unit produced goods and services for the commodity market. This split in the labour process has produced a split in the labour force roughly along sexual lines — women into the domestic unit, men into industry. The latter is the unit of capitalist production, the former is the unit of reproduction for capital.[13]

At stake behind the fate of the Earnshaw family in *Wuthering Heights* is the transformation of the family in society into an ideological apparatus for the orderly management of social subjectivity, in a world constantly destabilized by the uncontrolled movement of capital. As the sadism of control functions alongside, and is complementary to, the anarchy of desire, so the careful reproduction of social relations operates alongside the unplanned momentum of profit. Thus, Heathcliff is both worker *and* capitalist, an image of the real and contradictory *relation* between capitalist and worker that *is* capitalism; he is an image of the worker catalysed into a productive force that actually works against itself. Emerging from the position of a labourer in the family economy, his working-class rage becomes the obverse of a fiercely capitalist, anarchic 'productivity'. Figuring the anarchic movement of 'productive' capital, and the ironic potency of the worker catalysed by capital, he rages through the social universe, revolutionizing previous social relations, abolishing obsolescent property formations and building new ones, and, ultimately, destroying the ground from under himself.

Thus, the problem of managing this energy is part of what is imagined in the narrative that develops from Heathcliff's introduction into the Earnshaw family up to its final reorganization. For the productive genie conjured up by capital, through its relation to the worker, is also a spectre that haunts it. Because the working class's productive power is at once generally indispensable (to capitalist productivity) and particularly bothersome (to capitalist stability), it must be managed. And so we have Nelly Dean, who, as domestic labourer as well as phallic Mother, must acknowledge the existence of this energy, and even finally cede its autonomy in a separate realm, but who must also work to defend the orderly reproduction of social relations through the family. She is indeed 'patriarchy's paradigmatic housekeeper', 'policing' the very important social realm that she represents. The contrast between the 'elemental' Heathcliff and the 'common sense' Nelly, which we have seen as figuring the antithetical demands of the Father's Desire and Law within the Oedipal scenario, is also affiliated to — and affiliates that scenario itself with — the centrifugal sociohistorical momentum of capital. It is capital that continually divides the social world, wrenching the productive energies it needs from the family, which, now emptied of its own economic power, becomes a means for reproducing appropriate working subjects:

The separation of the household from the means of production has had profound consequences for the family unit in the bourgeois epoch. For it is this separation that has placed the domestic unit beyond the exercise of the law of value. The restless momentum of capital operating within the industrial process provides the impetus for the constant transformation of the organization of labour and technology that has been a hallmark of the capitalist system. The domestic labour force, having no direct relation with capital, is only affected by this development peripherally and has not undergone any significant structural alteration in the organization of its labour process throughout the entire capitalist epoch.[14]

Heathcliff and Nelly's position in *Wuthering Heights* as *surrogate* father and mother, as part of the 'domestic labour force' which Heathcliff leaves but Nelly remains within, makes explicit the text's internal association of the 'restless momentum of capital' with the restless momentum of Oedipal desire, an unavoidable association even within the single and singular word 'Penistone'. The antagonism between Heathcliff and Nelly's phallo-eccentric and phallic maternal roles, and between their opposed strategies of qualitative, metaphoric satisfaction versus incremental, 'realistic' ambition, is further overdetermined by the contradiction between furious socio-economic productivity and pacific domestic tranquillity. The phallic mother as capitalism's paradigmatic domestic labourer is what the text *invents to solve its multiple problems*, showing us that neither Capital nor the Father has actually to be — and in fact would rather not be — present in the family for this institution to function quite nicely on their behalf.

But the membrane that separates the sphere of social reproduction from the sphere of social production, the ideological factory from the commodity factory, is always too permeable. The male and female subjects that migrate across it continually tend to bring the disruptive need for dynamic individual growth into the family, and the disruptive need for collective support into the market-place. In fact, this strict separation can only represent the impossible Anglo-capitalist dream of ideological, flowing from

familial, stability. And part of *Wuthering Heights*'s peculiar
power derives from its reluctance to imagine any stable,
'compromise' resolution that would deny the integrity and
tenacity of the psycho-sexual and socio-ideological tensions
that constitute the novel. The final sense of precariousness
that the text projects — the sense that all of this can
happen again, that the energies which Heathcliff unleashed
are doomed repeatedly to intervene in, and transform, the
everyday family world — is a recognition both of the
inevitable, unforseeable return of repressed phallic desire
within the Oedipal family, and of the constant cycle of
disruption and renewal that capitalism — not the elements
— imposes on the social family.

Conclusion: The Text in Crisis

In formal terms, the narrative dynamic of *Wuthering Heights* generates this structure:

Heights: Heathcliff-Cathy

Grange: Nelly, Hareton-Cathy

Yet this structure is itself not purely 'formal', nor a reflection of some 'elemental', metaphysical division of the mind/cosmos. It is, rather, a peculiarly 'produced', imperfect and imaginary resolution, worked out in terms of a carefully specified textual conflict, to some of the real contradictions constituting the family in patriarchal, industrial, Anglo-capitalist society. This family must produce and feed on productive social, and irrepressible Oedipal, energies without being affected by them; it must be a stable site for the reproduction of social subjects in a tumultuous world dominated by the anarchy of production; and, to say the same thing, it must incorporate a subtly sadistic control over a sublimated anarchy of desire. For it is the controlled reproduction of anarchic production that urges the sadistic control of anarchic desire. It is on this site, managed by the phallic mother as paradigmatic ideological labourer, that the social and psycho-sexual subjects of this novel — beginning with Cathy and ending with Heathcliff — are torn apart.

To say that the resolution of psycho-sexual and social

contradictions is imagined in this text is not to 'reduce' the novel's significance in any way, but to raise it to its inscribed power. For the point of *Wuthering Heights* is not to reveal the metaphysics of the elements, but to work out the structural possibilities for a family which is revolutionized as a socio-ideological institution by the pressures of insurgent capital, even as its psycho-sexual subjects are rent by the pressures of phallic desire. The point of *Wuthering Heights* — even of *Wuthering Heights* — is to manage a crisis of self and society peculiar to a world dominated by the anarchy of capital as well as by the law of the father — a world, that is, not yet of our own creating.

Notes

Preface

1 This point is made in Fredric Jameson, 'Interview', *Diacritics*, 12, 3 (fall 1982), p. 88, and in Jameson and James H. Kavanagh, 'The Weakest Link: Marxism in Literary Studies', in Bertell Ollman and Edward Vernoff, eds, *The Left Academy: Marxist Scholarship on American Campuses*, vol. 2 (New York: Praeger, 1984), p. 9.

2 Ursula K. LeGuin, *The Dispossessed* (New York: Avon, 1975), pp. 258–9.

Introduction: *Wuthering Heights* and Critical Method

1 This is not meant to disregard her poetry, but it is surely *Wuthering Heights* that has established the literary Emily Brontë whom we know. For an excellent study of Emily Brontë's poetry, see Margaret Homans, *Woman Writers and Poetic Identity* (Princeton: Princeton University Press, 1980), pp. 104–62.

2 From an unsigned review in the *Examiner*, 8 January 1848, quoted in Miriam Allott, ed., *The Brontës: The Critical Heritage* (London: Routledge and Kegan Paul, 1974). p. 220.

3 From an unsigned review in the *Britannia*, 15 January 1848, quoted in Allott, *The Brontës*, p. 224.

4 'Biographical Notice of Ellis and Acton Bell', taken from the second (1850) edition of *Wuthering Heights*, as produced in Emily Brontë, *Wuthering Heights*, ed. Hilda Marsden and Ian Jack (Oxford: Oxford University Press, 1976), p. 436. All subsequent citations from *Wuthering Heights*, and from Charlotte's prefaces thereto, are taken from this edition and referenced by page number in the body of the text.

5 From the *Examiner*, 8 January 1848, quoted in Allott, *The Brontës*, p. 222.

6 From a review by Sidney Dobell in the *Palladium*, September 1850, quoted in Allott, *The Brontës*, p. 278. Dobell surmised that 'Currer, Ellis, and Acton Bell' were the same female author: 'Every word she utters is female. Not feminine, but female ... Though she spoke in thunder, and had the phrase and idiom of Achilles, she cannot *think* in a beard' (p. 277). For a detailed discussion of the critical double standard that operated for women writers, see chapter II of Elaine Showalter's important study, *A Literature of Their Own* (Princeton: Princeton University Press, 1976). Showalter discusses the reviews of the Brontës on pp. 90—3. Curiously, Showalter uses a quote from G.H. Lewes, another critic of th 1850s, to help establish a very different kind of distinction between 'feminine' and 'female' writing. Tom Winnifrith in *The Brontës and their Background* (London: Macmillan, 1973), pp. 110—38, gives a detailed discussion of the Brontë reviewers.

7 William M. Sale, jun.'s comment in his edition of *Wuthering Heights*, rev. edn (New York: Norton, Norton Critical Editions, 1972), p. 278.

8 From Dobell, in the *Palladium*, quoted in Allott, *The Brontës*, p. 279.

9 *Early Victorian Novelists* (Indianapolis: Bobbs-Merrill, 1935), p. 173.

10 Mark Schorer, 'Introduction', in his edition of *Wuthering Heights* (New York: Holt, Rinehart and Winston, 1950), p. ix.

11 Ibid, p. ix.

12 Dorothy Van Ghent, *The English Novel: Form and Function* (New York: Holt, Rinehart and Winston, 1953), p. 156.

13 *The Brontës* (2 vols, Essex, Longman House, 1974), 2: 42—3.

14 *Critical Practice* (London: Methuen, 1980), pp. 7ff. Belsey also succinctly explains that what is at work in such criticism is an empiricist-idealist *couple*. To elaborate: the expressive-realist assumption seems, and when recognized claims to be, staunchly empiricist, since it insists that the text is grounded in a toe-stubbing 'reality'; but this empiricism turns quickly into a rather more vague idealism, when the hard 'reality' that grounds the text turns out to be a version of the authorial 'mind' — a ghostly presence, hidden by yet pervading the text, *and* when the text turns out to be something implicitly 'unreal', or at least 'less' real and transparent. The point is not to deny that there are 'realities' upon which what we call the literary text depends, but that the first realities we confront, and cannot simply 'pass through', are the very real ensemble of procedures

and discourses that make the text visible in a specific form in the first place, and the very real ensemble of material signifiers that then comes into view — neither of which is reducible or transparent to some anterior 'ur'-reality. The problem with 'expressive realism' is not that it insists on, but that it has too poor a concept of, the real.

15 *Lenin and Philosophy* (New York: Monthly Review Press, 1971), pp. 162—5. I should suggest that Althusser's use of 'representing' is to be taken less in the usual sense of 'symbolizing', than in the sense of 'present[ing], produc[ing], or perform[ing] (a play, etc.)', 'act[ing] the part of', or even 'speak[ing] and act[ing] for by duly conferred authority, as an ambassador for his country or a legislator for his constituents' (*Webster's New World Dictionary*, Second College Edition, s.v. 'represent').

'Imaginary' here does not mean 'unreal', and does not designate some Coleridgean quality of the aesthetic mind, but derives from the Lacanian designation of a specific stage or instance in the constitution of the self. In Lacanian theory, the 'Imaginary' is a stage prior to linguistic competence and prior to the differentiation of sexual identity, where the child begins to find a coherent sense of self by observing his/her bodily *image* (in a mirror, in relation to the body of the mother). This is contraposed with the 'Symbolic' instance which is inaugurated by the recognition of the interfering presence of the phallic father. At this stage, the child simultaneously enters the Oedipal conflict, acquires linguistic competence, and comes under the sway of patriarchal Law; at this point, too, the human subject begins to identify him/herself as a sexed subject playing a certain role in the Oedipal drama, and as a linguistic subject, occupying a certain position in language. In the Symbolic order, the human subject is also always kept at a distance from what Lacan calls the 'Real', the domain of all that exceeds or lies beyond linguistic signification. For a more complete exposition of the Althusserian theory of ideology, see James H. Kavanagh, 'Marxism's Althusser: Toward a Politics of Literary Theory', *Diacritics*, 12, 1 (spring, 1982), 25—45. The Lacanian theory of the Imaginary order is explained in length in Anthony Wilden, ed., *The Language of the Self*, by Jacques Lacan (New York: Dell, Delta Books, (1975) pp. 159—77; in Anika Lemaire, *Jacques Lacan* (London: Routledge and Kegan Paul, 1977), pp. 60—1, 177—8; and in Juliet Mitchell, *Psychoanalysis and Feminism* (New York: Vintage, 1975), pp. 392ff. It is more tersely (but helpfully) related to Althusserian theory in Belsey, *Critical Practice*, pp. 64—5. Fredric Jameson carefully articulates Lacanian theory and Marxism in 'Imaginary and Symbolic in Lacan:

Marxism, Psychoanalysis, and the Problem of the Subject', *Literature and Psychoanalysis: The Question of Reading: Otherwise*, special issue of *Yale French Studies*, nos 55—6 (1977), pp. 338—95, and in the first chapter of *The Political Unconscious: Narrative as a Socially Symbolic Act* (Ithaca: Cornell University Press, 1981). Terry Eagleton's chapter on psychoanalysis in *Literary Theory: An Introduction* (Oxford: Basil Blackwell, 1983), pp. 151—93, gives an extraordinarily lucid account of Lacanian and classical Freudian psychoanalytic theory.

16 The primary meaning of 'articulate' as used here is not 'to speak clearly', but 'to fit together well', 'to order carefully', or 'to correlate'; and even more specifically, 'to put together by joints', as we might speak of a 'well-articulated' chair (*Webster's New World Dictionary*, s.v. 'articulate'). Thus language is a semiotic system which helps the individual to make the 'fit' between self and society.

17 On the character of literary-ideological 'work' and the characteristics of the literary 'mode of production', see chapters 2 and 3 of Terry Eagleton, *Criticism and Ideology* (London: New Left Books, 1976).

18 A 'seme' is an elementary unit of signification, the smallest irreducible unit of meaning, and thus a fundamental building block of a semiotic system. 'Symptomatic reading' (*lecture symptomale*) refers to a process of reading a text modelled on the way an analyst 'reads' the peculiar associations, inconsistencies and silences of the analysand's utterances as symptomatic of unconscious conflicts. See Louis Althusser, *For Marx* (New York: Vintage, 1970), pp. 68—70; Althusser and Etienne Balibar, *Reading Capital* (London: New Left Books, 1975), pp. 32—3; Pierre Macherey, *A Theory of Literary Production* (London: Routledge and Kegan Paul, 1978); and Macherey and Etienne Balibar, 'Literature as an Ideological Form: Some Marxist Hypotheses', *Praxis*, 5 (1980).

19 Ibid., p. 57. For further comment on this powerful analogy between the analysand's account of the dream and the critic's account of the text, see James H. Kavanagh, 'To the Same Defect: Toward a Critique of the Ideology of the Aesthetic', in *The Bucknell Review* 27, 1 (fall 1982), pp. 102—23, and id., 'Shakespeare in Ideology', in John Drakakis, ed., *Alternative Shakespeares* (London: Methuen, 1985).

20 'Editor's Preface to the New [1850] Edition of *Wuthering Heights*', p. 442.

21 'Cathexis' is Freud's word for a 'charge' of libidinal energy that, under the pressure of the ego's censorship, often becomes

fixated on a peculiar object — a displaced and contradictory version of the original object of desire. See Sigmund Freud, *A General Introduction to Psychoanalysis* (New York: Simon & Schuster, Pocket Books, 1972), pp. 368ff.

22 For a polemical account of various Marxist approaches to the novel (curiously side-tracked by discussions of Q.D. Leavis and Frank Kermode), see Ronald Frankenberg, 'Styles of Marxism: Styles of Criticism. *Wuthering Heights*: A Case Study', in Diana Laurenson, ed., *The Sociology of Literature: Applied Studies* (Keele: University of Keele, 1978), pp. 109—44.

23 'Emily Brontë: First of the Moderns', *Modern Quarterly Miscellany*, 1 (1947), pp. 94—115.

24 *Wuthering Heights* was first published in two volumes in December 1847, by Thomas Cautley Newby of London. The *Communist Manifesto* was commissioned in London in November 1847, and was printed (in German) in London in February 1848. The first English translation appeared in London in 1850.

25 'Emily Brontë: First of the Moderns', p. 98.

26 In 1812, when Patrick Brontë was in Hartshead, seventeen unemployed Yorkshire weavers were hung for taking part in demonstrations. Shelley helped to raise money for their families. This incident is mentioned in Annette T. Rubinstein, *The Great Tradition in English Literature from Shakespeare to Shaw* (2 vols, New York: Monthly Review Press, 1969), 2: 529.

27 See Wilson, 'Emily Brontë: First of the Moderns', pp. 99—100; John Lock and Canon W.T. Dixon, *A Man of Sorrow: The Life, Letters, and Times of the Reverend Patrick Brontë* (London: Ian Hodgkins, 1979), pp. 102—3; and Winifred Gérin, *Emily Brontë* (Oxford: Oxford University Press, 1971), pp. 147—8. Lock and Dixon's book is pure hagiography of the father, and treats all this reactionary posturing with an air of bemusement.

28 *The Brontës*, 1: 11.

29 Gérin, *Emily Brontë*, p. 147.

30 Lock and Dixon, *A Man of Sorrow*, p. 369.

31 *The Madwoman in the Attic: The Woman Writer and the Nineteenth-Century Literary Imagination* (New Haven: Yale University Press, 1979), p. 14.

32 'Parapraxis' is the psychoanalytic word for symptomatic slips of the tongue or pen.

33 This quote, including '[sic]', is taken exactly from Gérin, *Emily Brontë*, pp. 147—8. Gérin chooses to call attention to the use of 'raped' for 'rapt', but not to other misspellings, such as 'irristable'. Lock and Dixon reproduce the same quote, but give the word as 'wrapt', with no indication that they have edited it.

34 Wilson, 'Emily Brontë: First of the Moderns', p. 110.
35 See the chapter on *Wuthering Heights*, in Kettle, *An Introduction to the English Novel* (2 vols, London: Hillary House, 1951), 1: 138—53.
36 'Emily Brontë: First of the Moderns', p. 118.
37 David Musselwhite, '*Wuthering Heights*: The Unacceptable Text', in Francis Barker, John Coombes, Peter Hulme, David Musselwhite and Richard Osborne, eds, *Literature, Society and the Sociology of Literature* (Essex: University of Essex, 1977), pp. 154—60. Francis Barker, '*Wuthering Heights* and the Real Conditions', *Red Letters*, 3 (autumn 1976), pp. 10—11.

 I cannot hope to supply adequate references for the notion of 'textuality', developed by French theoreticians Roland Barthes and Jacques Derrida, which is at the centre of so much contemporary post-structuralist critical discourse. This word is meant to register both the sense in which all meaning is produced within a specific field of material signifiers (words, images, gestures, etc.) that tend to be arranged in text-like systems, and the sense in which those signifiers produce meaning through a potentially infinite process of reciprocal differentiation (what deconstructionists would call a play of difference and deferral) that has no stable ground or centre, and can only be given a provisional systemic order. For further explication and reference, see Michael Ryan, *Marxism and Deconstruction: A Critical Articulation* (Baltimore: The John Hopkins University Press, 1982), pp. 22ff; Gayatri Chakravorty Spivak, 'Introduction', in Jacques Derrida, *Of Grammatology* (Baltimore: The Johns Hopkins University Press, 1976); Jonathan Culler, *On Deconstruction* (Ithaca: Cornell University Press, 1984); Christopher Norris, *Deconstruction: Theory and Practice* (London: Methuen, 1982); Ann Jefferson, 'Structuralism and Post-Structuralism', in Ann Jefferson and David Robey, eds, *Modern Literary Theory: A Comparative Introduction* (Totowa, N.J.: Barnes and Noble, 1982), pp. 104ff; and Terry Eagleton, *Literary Theory*, pp. 132ff. See also note 14, this chapter.
38 *Myths of Power: A Marxist Study of the Brontës* (London: Macmillan, 1975), pp. 98—122.
39 Ibid., p. 119.
40 A phrase that Eagleton coins in his *Criticism and Ideology*, and makes liberal use of in chapters 4 and 5.
41 Id., *Myths of Power*, p. 116.
42 'Overdetermination' is a concept imported into Marxist literary theory from psychoanalysis, where it identifies the process through which a dream-image is constructed from multiple unconscious sources, from a 'multiplicity of determinations',

each of which distorts the image in a particular way. This concept underlies Freud's analysis of 'condensation' and 'displacement' — the techniques of dream-work whereby the dream constructs is peculiar images by continually fusing different, even contradictory, representations ('condensation'), or by transferring the libidinal charge associated with a certain object onto a seemingly inappropriate stand-in. See also Eagleton, *Literary Theory*, pp. 151—93, where these techniques of 'dream-work' are explained quite clearly. For further discussion of these concepts in relation to Marxist theory, see Althusser, 'Contradiction and Overdetermination', in *For Marx*; Macherey and Balibar, 'Literature as an Ideological Form'; Kavanagh, 'Marxism's Althusser'; Fredric Jameson, *The Political Unconscious*. In Freud, see *Jokes and their Relation to the Unconscious* (New York: Norton, 1960), pp. 162—3.

43 *Emily Brontë*, pp. 225—6.

44 *Myths of Power*, p. 120.

45 Belsey, *Critical Practice*, p. 61.

46 The 'subject-position' discussed here is not exactly 'author', 'reader' or 'character'. It is none and all of these — it is the virtual site that provides the *condition* for making such distinctions, 'the position from which the text is most "obviously" intelligible' (Ibid., p. 57). See also Eagleton, *Literary Theory*, pp. 119—21.

47 Althusser, *Lenin and Philosophy*, p. 171.

48 Ibid., pp. 171—5. For more on the ideological and literary constitution of subjectivity, see Belsey, *Critical Practice*, pp. 56ff., and Kavanagh, 'Marxism's Althusser', pp. 29ff. Hereafter, I shall use 'interpellation' and 'constitutive address' interchangeably.

49 Althusser, *For Marx*, p. 233.

50 Ibid., pp. 233—4.

51 *The Madwoman in the Attic*, pp. 248—308.

52 Harold Bloom argues that the literary tradition is less a progression of benign influences than a series of quasi-Oedipal struggles, in which younger poets are engaged in a continual love-hate battle with their literary 'fathers'. Bloom writes of this combat as an 'agon', the Greek term for an athletic contest, and also for the conflict of characters in a drama. The classic statement of this argument is in his *The Anxiety of Influence* (New York: Oxford University Press, 1973). Gilbert and Gubar's debt to Bloom is apparent throughout *The Madwoman in the Attic*, and their own agonistic transformation of it is dealt with especially on pp. 45ff.

53 Ibid., p. 295.

54 Ibid., p. 303.
55 *A Future for Astyanax* (Boston: Little, Brown, 1976), pp. 189—229. Gilbert and Gubar frequently cite this study.

Chapter 1 Patriarchal Law and the Anarchy of Desire

1 *Fables of Aggression: Wyndham Lewis, the Modernist as Fascist* (Berkeley: University of California Press, 1979), pp. 9—12.
2 Ibid., p. 10.
3 In *Ideology and the Image* (Bloomington: Indiana University Press, 1981), pp. 96ff, Bill Nichols has an excellent discussion of how logical paradox helps to constitute narrative suspense, and even aesthetic pleasure. As we shall see below, *Wuthering Heights* is in part structured by the paradoxical injunction: 'In order to have the object of desire, you must forgo it. But if you forgo the object of desire, then you cannot have it.' This is reflected in Cathy's paradoxical attitude towards marrying Heathcliff: 'My love for Heathcliff is metaphysical and timeless, not real and historical; it is not "marriageable". But if I don't "realize" it and marry him, I will lose him.' Eagleton deals with this contradictory attitude of Cathy's, without the emphasis on logical contradiction, in *Myths and Power: A Marxist Study of the Brontës* (London: Macmillan, 1975), pp. 101—2.
4 See Heathcliff's 'You know you lie to say I have killed you' (p. 196), and 'I have not broken your heart — *you* have broken it — and in breaking it, you have broken mine. So much the worse for me that I am strong' (p. 198).
5 Carol Jacobs, '*Wuthering Heights*: At the Threshold of Interpretation', *Boundary 2*, 7, 3 (spring 1979), p. 68.
6 In psychoanalytic theory, 'sublimation' is the basis of all cultural activity, the process by which the ego redirects libidinal sexual drives into socially valued, seemingly non-sexual ('sublime') activities. In this way, libidinal energies are allowed a certain indirect fulfilment, consistent with cultural and ethical constraints.
7 The standard statement on the book image can be found in Robert C. McKibben, 'The Image of the Book in *Wuthering Heights*', *Nineteenth-Century Fiction*, 15, 2 (September 1960), 159—69.
8 Sandra Gilbert and Susan Gubar, *The Madwoman in the Attic: The Woman Writer and the Nineteenth-Century Literary Imagination* (New Haven: Yale University Press, 1979), p. 14.
9 It is also worth keeping in mind, while reading this nightmare sermon, the discussion of the Brontë family's religious politics in David Wilson, 'Emily Brontë: First of the Moderns' (*Modern*

Quarterly Miscellany, 1 (1947)), especially his discussion of the Reverend Jabez Bunting, the hellfire-and-brimstone Super-intendent Minister of the Halifax Circuit and later President of the Methodist Conference, who 'damned the Luddites with "bell, book and candle" . . . refused to allow burial rites to be read over Methodist participants who were killed in the riots . . . [and] excommunicat[ed] ministers who identified themselves with the Radicals or the Chartists' (ibid., p. 99).

10 See especially Wade Thompson, 'Infanticide and Sadism in *Wuthering Heights*', in Jean-Pierre Petit, ed., *Emily Brontë: A Critical Anthology* (Harmondsworth: Penguin, 1973), pp. 193–204, where most of the following examples are noted.

11 Ibid., p. 194 'Without the care of their mothers' is an important phrase. Thompson makes much of the parallel with the Brontë family: 'we may note that the children in Wuthering Heights, like the children in the Brontë household, are left to fend for themselves in early life without the love or protection of their mothers.' Gilbert and Gubar also comment that 'Catherine may well need a mother', and that Hindley and Frances seem to her like oppressive step-parents (*The Madwoman in the Attic*, p. 269).

12 G.D. Klingopulos, 'The Novel as Dramatic Poem (II): *Wuthering Heights*', *Scrutiny*, 17, 4 (September 1947), 284–5.

13 See Sigmund Freud, *A General Introduction to Psychoanalysis* (New York: Simon & Schuster, Pocket Books, 1972) pp. 182, 369ff; see also the discussion, particularly relevant to literary analysis, in his book *Jokes and their Relation to the Unconscious* (New York: Norton, 1960), *passim*. 'Displacement' is closely related to 'condensation'. See introduction, note 42.

14 *The Daughter's Seduction* (Ithaca: Cornell University Press, 1982), pp. 77–8. 'Disavowal' or 'denial' is used here (as an equivalent for Freud's *Verleungnung*) in the specific psycho-analytic sense of the refusal of an unpleasant fact of uncon-scious life, a refusal whose specific characteristics mark it as a desperate defence against, and therefore confirmation of, that fact. The word is initially used by Freud to describe the male's response to the 'traumatic perception' of the woman's 'castra-tion', the mark of her radical *otherness* (ibid., p. 18).

Gallop's book, which I use as an important resource for the following discussion, is itself a quite specific, even idiosyncratic, interpretation of and confrontation with recent currents in post-Lacanian French feminist thought. English translations of some of the primary sources can be found in: 'French Feminist Theory', *Signs*, 7 (autumn 1981), a special issue that includes Cixous, Irigaray and Kristeva; Elaine Marks and Isabelle de

Courtivron, eds, *New French Feminisms: An Anthology* (Amherst: University of Massachusetts Press, 1980). Other commentaries and critiques include: Toril Moi, *Sexual/Textual Politics: A Study of Feminist Literary Theory* (London: Methuen, 1985); id., 'Textual Politics', *Diacritics*, 5, 4 (winter 1975); Elaine Marks, 'Review Essay: Women and Literature in France', *Signs*, 4 (1978), 832—42; Michele Richman, 'Sex and Signs: The Language of French Feminist Criticism', *Language and Style*, 13 (1980), 62—80; 'Feminist Readings: French Text, American Contexts', *Yale French Studies*, 62 (1981), a special issue, including essays by Shoshana Felman and Gayatri Chakravorty Spivak; 'Cherchez la Femme', *Diacritics*, 12, 2 (summer 1982), also a special issue.

15 Cited in Gallop, *The Daughter's Seduction*, p. 74. This characterization can be misleading, since the female is not the simple inversion of the male 'Oedipal' complex.

16 Ibid., pp. 70—1. *Wuthering Heights*, pp. 30—1.

17 Gallop, *The Daughter's Seduction*, p. 76, citing and commenting on Irigaray. *Pace* ibid., pp. 77—8, there are some things it is best to state precisely at all times: this discussion is not meant (by me, nor I think by Irigaray or Gallop) as any kind of argument for physically consummating father-daughter incest, but an analysis of the confusing enough conditions and effects of that incest as it always already occurs (or is *wished*, which is the same thing on this site) in the unconscious, and a 'calling into question [of] the law with which [the father] drapes his desire, and his sex (organ)' (Irigaray, quoted in ibid., p. 77).

18 'Penetralium' is Emily Brontë's mistaken singular for the plural noun 'penetralia' (the correct singular is 'penetrale'), defined by *The American Heritage Dictionary* (New York, 1970) as '1) the innermost parts of a building; especially the sanctuary of a temple. 2) Innermost or hidden parts; recesses: *the penetralia of the soul*'. 'Penates' are the Roman gods of the household. 'Penetralium', 'penates' and 'penetrate' all derive ultimately from the Latin word *penus* meaning 'the interior of a house'. 'Penis' is from a different root which never appears in this text, although virtually every other basal morpheme 'pen' does, making Emily Brontë's 'pen' a highly overdetermined signifying unit.

19 Cecil W. Davies, 'A Reading of *Wuthering Heights*', in Petit, *Emily Brontë*, p. 283.

20 Thus, I find speculation, like that of Eric Solomon in 'The Incest Theme in *Wuthering Heights*' (*Nineteenth-Century Fiction*, 14, 1 (June 1959), pp. 80—3, that Heathcliff 'could possibly be Earnshaw's illegitimate offspring' and therefore

'really' Cathy's blood-brother, to be entirely irrelevant to the incest *fantasy* that drives this text. The unconscious displacement of the father prominently displayed in the symbolic order — the letter — of this text goes entirely unnoticed in the literal-minded search for Heathcliff and Cathy's sibling consanguinity, which only repeats an avoidance mechanism.

21 'Anaclitic' (from the Greek *anaklinein* [αυακ λωεω], 'to lean upon') is a term from psychoanalytic theory used to describe how the sexual libido leans up against, or attaches itself to, other — primarily self-preservative — instincts. See Freud, *A General Introduction to Psychoanalysis*, pp. 433—5.

22 This term is from Freud's discussion (in 'The Antithetical Sense of Primal Words' in *Freud on Creativity and the Unconscious* (New York: Harper and Row, 1958), pp. 55—62) of words that carry contrary meanings. These words were for Freud an analogue of the dream-image, which fuses contradictory representations through the unconscious 'dream-work' of 'condensation' mentioned above. See Freud, *Jokes*, pp. 173—5, and *A General Introduction to Psychoanalysis*, p. 369.

23 I reintroduce here, in another form, a difference between two inflections of the father's demand (one a demand for submission to the father's Law, the other a demand for submission to the father's body), and take Gallop's point that patriarchy refers to the rule of the father's *Law*, and is 'grounded in the uprightness of the father' (*The Daughter's Seduction*, pp. 74—5). I emphasize that these are two 'antithetical' inflections of the *same* complex demand, and thus form what we might call a difference without a distinction.

Chapter 2 The Phallic Mother and the Sadism of Control

1 For a clever and naively moralistic interpretation of Nelly as the 'villain' of the novel, see James Hafley, 'The Villain in *Wuthering Heights*', *Nineteenth-Century Fiction*, 23, 3 (December 1958), pp. 199—215; reprinted in Richard Lettis and William E. Morris, eds, *A Wuthering Heights Handbook* (New York: Odyssey Press, 1961).

2 See Bill Nichols's discussion of narrative diegesis in *Ideology and the Image* (Bloomington: Indiana University Press, 1981), pp. 82ff, and Terry Eagleton's discussion of narrative theory in *Literary Theory: An Introduction* (Oxford: Basil Blackwell, 1983), pp. 105ff.

3 Nelly is the principal — that is, most important — narrator, but Lockwood is the primary narrator — that is, the one who communicates directly with the reader.

4   Sandra Gilbert and Susan Gubar, *The Madwoman in the Attic: The Woman Writer and the Nineteenth-Century Literary Imagination* (New Haven: Yale University Press, 1979), pp. 290–1, 295.

5   *Wuthering Heights*, p. 46. This division endures in the text, and involves both sympathy and antagonism by association; Nelly is closer to Hindley than to Heathcliff *or* Cathy: 'I own I did not like her, after her infancy was past' (p. 82); 'I confess this blow [Hindley's death] was greater to me than the shock of Mrs. Linton's [Cathy's] death: ancient associations lingered around my heart. I sat down in the porch and wept as for a blood relation' (p. 228).

6   See Roland Barthes, 'Introduction to the Structural Analysis of Narrative', in Stephen Heath, ed., *Image-Music-Text: Roland Barthes* (New York: Hill and Wang, 1977), pp. 79–124.

7   Nelly in fact calls herself Hindley's 'foster sister' (p. 81) and calls Hindley her 'foster brother' (p. 229). This is an accurate contemporary usage, according to the *OED*, since her mother had nursed them both — that is, they too had shared the childhood pleasures of a 'dairy woman'.

8   *The Madwoman in the Attic*, p. 290.

9   Ibid.

10 As a male, of course, Heathcliff has more chance of changing his 'eligibility'.

11 *The Madwoman in the Attic*, p. 290.

12 Ibid., p. 291.

13 Ibid.

14 *The Daughter's Seduction* (Ithaca: Cornell University Press, 1982), pp. 117–18.

15 See introduction, note 15.

16 Gallop, *The Daughter's Seduction*, p. 76.

17 Gilbert and Gubar, *The Madwoman in the Attic*, pp. 281–2.

18 'Transference' is the psychoanalytic term for the way a patient transfers on to the analyst the unconscious conflicts associated with other — usually parental — figures. This phenomenon threatens to undermine the analysis, because it makes the analyst a participant in the analysand's unconscious problematic, and the analytic situation a scene where habitual strategies for avoiding difficult problems are repeated.

19 Gallop, *The Daughter's Seduction*, p. 114–15.

20 Gilbert and Gubar, *The Madwoman in the Attic*, p. 294. Heathcliff would be, in Showalter's terms, a version of the aggressive, 'brutish' woman's man — a category that, for her, has a dual ('impossibly pious, impossibly oversexed') aspect. We might say that *Wuthering Heights* figures this ambivalence itself in the

Heathcliff-Edgar dualism. Showalter also emphasizes the sense in which such heroes are 'not so much [female authors'] ideal lovers as their projected egos [,] . . . the product of female fantasies that are much more concerned with power and authority than with romance'. Thus, many of these heroes are 'extremely aggressive in bourgeois economic terms', and 'much of the wish-fulfilment in the feminine novel comes from women wishing they were men, with the greater freedom and range masculinity confers.' (See Elaine Showalter, *A Literature of Their Own* (Princeton: Princeton University Press, 1976), pp. 133—52; Heathcliff is mentioned on p. 141.) This is certainly a cogent point, and a necessary correction of previous emphases, though I would want to put it that, in this wish-fulfilment at least, it is impossible to extricate questions of power from questions of romance.

21 Gallop, *The Daughter's Seduction*, pp. 37—9. These remarks are part of Gallop's characterization of Lacan.
22 Ibid., p. 20.
23 Gilbert and Gubar, *The Madwoman in the Attic*, p. 280.

Chapter 3 The Contradictory Articulation of the Narrative

1 Sandra Gilbert and Susan Gubar, *The Madwoman in the Attic: The Woman Writer and the Nineteenth-Century Literary Imagination* (New Haven: Yale University Press, 1979), pp. 282—7.
2 Ibid., p. 272. Leo Bersani, in *A Future for Astyanax* (Boston: Little, Brown, 1976), pp. 7ff, has a useful critical discussion of recent 'philosophical pastorals of pre-Oedipal desire'. Gilbert and Gubar might be said to make of *Wuthering Heights* a prose pastoral of post-Oedipal gyandry/androgyny.
3 Charles Percy Sanger, 'The Structure of *Wuthering Heights*', in Thomas A. Vogler, ed., *Twentieth Century Interpretations of Wuthering Heights* (Englewood Cliffs N.J.: Prentice-Hall, 1968) p. 16. Also quoted in Gilbert and Gubar, *The Madwoman in the Attic*, p. 282.
4 Jane Gallop, *The Daughter's Seduction* (Ithaca: Cornell University Press, 1982), pp. 142—3. Gallop is here critically presenting the work of the French feminist, Hélène Cixous. See also chapter 2, note 18.
5 Ibid., p. 146.
6 It is unclear what Nelly knows about Heathcliff's whereabouts during this conversation with Cathy; even what she *says* she knows is ambiguous. Nelly at first asserts to Lockwood that she thought Heathcliff had 'walked through to the barn' (p. 94)

before Cathy entered, and claims to have noticed his presence on the other side of the wall only during Cathy's speech, at the moment when he got up to leave. But when Catherine does come in, Nelly seems surprised at Heathcliff's lack of reaction during the following prefatory exchange: ' "Where's Heathcliff?" she said, interrupting me. "About his work in the stable," was my answer. He did not contradict me; perhaps he had fallen into a doze' (p. 95). Nelly's response here is in an imperative mood: besides being a false answer to Cathy's question, it is an implicit message to Heathcliff that he *should not* reveal his presence.

7   On the two possibilities of the maternal symbolic see Gallop, *The Daughter's Seduction*, p. 124: 'the imaginary is conservative and comforting, tends toward closure, and is disrupted by the symbolic. . . . It seems to me there are two kinds of maternals; one more conservative than the paternal symbolic, one less.' See also Anthony Wilden, ed., *The Language of the Self*, by Jacques Lacan (New York: Dell, Delta Books, 1975) pp. 159—77, and Juliet Mitchell, *Psychoanalysis and Feminism* (New York: Vintage, 1975), pp. 394ff.

8   The Lintons' position as the local gentry is most clearly marked when Cathy and Heathcliff are taken for robbers when caught peering into the Grange windows:

> The rascals knew that yesterday was my rent day; they thought to have me cleverly . . . To beard a magistrate in his strong-hold, and on the Sabbath, too! . . . [I] t is but a boy — yet the villain scowls so plainly in his face, would it not be a kindness to the country to hang him at once, before he shows his nature in his acts as well as features? (p. 61)

This is also where Heathcliff learns the clear class division between him and Cathy. When the Lintons recognize Cathy, they are amazed at 'Miss Earnshaw scouring the country with a gipsy!' (p. 61), and their cavalier ruthlessness turns to concern for her ('That's Miss Earnshaw! . . . and look how Skulker has bitten her — how her foot bleeds!' (p. 61)), while Heathcliff is sent packing as 'A wicked boy, at all events' (p. 62).

Chapter 4   The Daughter's Division

1   Jane Gallop, *The Daughter's Seduction*, (Ithaca: Cornell University Press, 1982), p. 144.
2   Ibid., p. 144. Gallop's citation is from Hélène Cixous and Catherine Clément, *La jeune née* (Paris: Union Générale d'Editions, Collection '10/18', 1975), p. 276.

3   Gallop, *The Daughter's Seduction*, p. 145.
4   Sandra Gilbert and Susan Gubar, *The Madwoman in the Attic: The Woman Writer and the Nineteenth-Century Literary Imagination* (New Haven: Yale University Press, 1979), p. 291.
5   'Elf-bolts' were stone arrowheads, relics of pre-historic cultures, which were thought by popular legend to be weapons that the fairies would shoot at cattle. See *Wuthering Heights*, Notes, p. 426.
6   The spelling of this word varies in the text; it sometimes appears with, and sometimes without, the final 'e'. Similarly, 'Crags' sometimes has one, sometimes two, 'g's.
7   Gilbert and Gubar, *The Madwoman in the Attic*, p. 295.

Chapter 5 The Limits of the Textual Ideology

1   Cathy does in fact give birth to a 'puny', two months premature infant (p. 201).
2   *Wuthering Heights*, p. 179. The primary meaning of 'slut' in the mid-nineteenth century is not sexual. It means a 'dirty, slovenly, or untidy' woman. The *OED* gives one 1848 usage that seems similar to a contemporary version of 'bag lady': 'Almshouses for sluts whose husbands died'. It does have a secondary meaning of 'a woman of low or loose character', although even this meaning would be extended to an 'impudent' young girl. 'Slattern', too, means 'slovenly or untidy', and seems not to have even a secondary sexual meaning (see the *OED*, s.v. 'slattern', 'slut').
3   This sympathy, we should remark, may occur in different forms for male and female readers. For the latter, any sympathy for Heathcliff would have to pass through his aspect as a 'phallo-cccentric' 'woman's man', as indicated above (see chapter 2). There is also a sense in which sympathy for Heathcliff passes through his association with the Heights, since, as Terry Eagleton points out, 'the novel's sympathies lie on balance with the Heights rather than the Grange' (*Myths of Power: A Marxist Study of the Brontës* (London: Macmillan, 1975), p. 117).

Chapter 6 The Abolition of Characters in 'the Name-of-the-Father, but . . . '

1   In fact, only under the terms of the Inheritance Act of 1833 (Edgar Linton and Linton Heathcliff die in 1801) would Heathcliff's claim to the Grange after his son's death supersede Catherine Linton's. Sanger thinks that Emily Brontë is working

on the more historically accurate basis of the pre—1833 laws, and that Heathcliff is illegally, though effectively, in possession of the Grange; Marsden and Jack in their edition think the novel assumes the 1833 law, giving Heathcliff's claim legal precedence over Cathy's (see Charles Percy Sanger, 'The Structure of *Wuthering Heights*', in Thomas A. Vogler, ed., *Twentieth Century Interpretations of Wuthering Heights* (Englewood Cliffs, N.J.: Prentice-Hall, 1968), pp. 22—4, and *Wuthering Heights*, pp. 497—9.

This could serve as a nice example of an unanswerable question about an authorial intention that is assumed to determine the meaning of the text. How can we know whether Emily Brontë 'really' meant to have this situation governed by the laws in force when she wrote the text, or those in force at the time of the narrated events?

2   Despite the apparent symmetry of the family combinations, the only final possibilities of union are asymmetrical: the new single family that results from the merger of the original two will *either* be predominantly Linton (Cathy with Linton, a match that is one-half Linton and one-quarter Earnshaw — Linton Heathcliff has no Earnshaw blood), *or* predominantly Earnshaw (Cathy with Hareton, one-half Earnshaw, one-quarter Linton — maintaining direct patrilineal Earnshaw descent).

3   I am working here with the distinction in modern speech-act theory between 'performative' and 'constative' discourses — between those designed to produce a specific effect on an audience and get something done, and those designed to inform an audience of certain facts. This distinction is not solid, and it becomes difficult to conceive of any discourse — and certainly any literary discourse — that is not in some sense 'performative'. See J.L. Austin, *How to Do Things with Words*, eds, J.O. Urmson and Marina Sbisà (2nd edn, Cambridge, Massachusetts: Harvard University Press, 1975), and Eagleton, *Literary Theory: An Introduction* (Oxford: Basil Blackwell, 1983), pp. 118—19.

Chapter 7   The Hol(e)y Family: Exiling Desire and Housekeeping Ideology

1   See Althusser's essay, 'Ideology and Ideological State Apparatuses', in his *Lenin and Philosophy* (New York: Monthly Review Press, 1971).

2   Wally Secombe, 'The Housewife and Her Labour under Capitalism', *New Left Review*, 83 (January-February 1973), pp. 5, 15. This controversial article intervenes in a complex debate

about the Marxist understanding of the economic 'productivity' of domestic labour — that is, in short, whether or not domestic labour produces surplus-value. I have tried to use the article's cogent characterization of what I understand as a real socio-historical *tendency* (within Anglo-capitalist societies) — but not necessarily an actual *state of affairs* — for the family to perform a predominantly ideological function, without addressing the specific issue of the 'productivity' or lack thereof, of whatever labour occurs within the family. Other interventions in this debate include: Margaret Benson, 'The Political Economy of Women's Liberation', *Monthy Review* (September 1969); Mariarosa Dalla Costa, *The Power of Women and the Subversion of the Community* (Bristol, England: Falling Wall Press, 1972); Peggy Morton, 'Women's Work is Never Done', *Women Unite* (Toronto: Canadian Women's Educational Press, 1972); Ira Gerstein, 'Domestic Work and Capitalism', *Radical America*, 7, 4 and 5 (July-October 1973); B. Magas, H. Wainwright, Margaret Coulson, ' "The Housewife and Her Labour under Capitalism" — A Critique', *New Left Review*, 89 (January-February 1975); Barbara Erenreich and Deirdre English, 'The Manufacture of Housework', *Socialist Revolution*, 5, 26 (October-December 1975); Jean Gardiner, 'Women's Domestic Labor', in Zillah R. Eisenstein, ed., *Capitalist Patriarchy and the Case for Socialist Feminism* (New York: Monthly Review Press, 1979, also in *New Left Review*, 89); Michèle Barrett, *Women's Oppression Today* (London: New Left Books, 1980); Michèle Barrett and Mary McIntosh, *The Anti-Social Family* (London: New Left Books, 1982).

3   *The Making of the English Working Class* (New York: Vintage, 1963), p. 334. See also E.J. Hobsbawm, *The Age of Revolution* (New York: Mentor, 1962), pp. 70—1.

4   Winifred Gérin, *The Brontës* (2 vols, Essex: Longman House, 1974), 1:9.

5   Cited in ibid., p. 11. The 'circumstances' to which Charlotte refers were, of course, the exclusionary privileges and elitism of the very ruling classes which Patrick Brontë, the ex-Irish peasant boy, fought so hard to defend: 'Even when his own destiny led him into [opposite] . . . paths, his heart yearned after the glory he had glimpsed at Cambridge. But without money a man could not get a commission, nor without influence enter politics' (ibid., p. 10).

6   Ibid., p. 12.

7   Sandra Gilbert and Susan Gubar, *The Madwoman in the Attic: The Woman Writer and the Nineteenth-Century Literary Imagination* (New Haven: Yale University Press, 1979), pp. 252—3.

8   Ibid., p. 252.
9   *Webster's New World Dictionary*, Second College Edition, s.v. 'stone'.
10   *OED*, s.v. 'Penistone'.
11   Ibid., s.v. 'penny'.
12   *Wuthering Heights*, Notes, p. 425
13   Secombe, 'The Housewife and Her Labour', pp. 5—6.
14   Ibid., p. 16. Secombe is here, it seems to me, exaggerating the actual stability of a family structure whose most important (and very real) function has been more, as I have suggested, that of an imaginary ideal. Among the working classes of even the most 'advanced' capitalist countries, the stable nuclear family has always been subject to severe disruptive pressures; and among the rural and urban working classes of many semi-dependent peripheral societies, it simply does not exist.

Index

Kristevan reading

- Lockwood literally + fig helpless Nelly's story —
(bound by it)
Nelly's linguistic sadism is oral; L's litet.
class distinction oral / literary

Kavenaugh does what say in no good —
talks about Nelly's words in
story not as producure thereof 42

intersubjective claustrophobia —
Heathcliff — extends family (Nelly)
Cathy's anorexia
unquiet sleepers / sublimity
Satan - Dracula - undead claustrophobia —
no minor reflection